THE ILLUSTRATIONS

OF

W.HEATH ROBINSON

'He did not come to woo her, he said, he had only come to hear the
wisdom of the princess.' Illustration for *Hans Andersen's Fairy Tales*
(Constable & Co. Ltd., 1913)

THE ILLUSTRATIONS

OF

W. HEATH ROBINSON

A COMMENTARY AND BIBLIOGRAPHY BY GEOFFREY C. BEARE

LONDON: WERNER SHAW LTD
1983

For David and Jonathan

© Geoffrey C. Beare, 1983
ISBN 0 907961 02 9

Printed and bound in Great Britain for
the publishers, Werner Shaw Limited,
26 Charing Cross Road (Suite 34), London
WC2H 0HY by Biddles Limited, Guildford,
Surrey. Typeset in Janson and Times by
Alacrity Phototypesetters, Banwell Castle,
Weston-super-Mare. Jacket design by Alan Downs

CONTENTS

Acknowledgements

One of the great pleasures of writing this book has been that it has brought me into contact with Heath Robinson's children. My particular thanks are due to Oliver Robinson, for writing the Introduction and for providing me with much information on magazine publishing, and the history of the National Magazine Company. Also to his sister, Joan Brinsmead, for lending me many of her father's letters and press cuttings, and to Alan, Quentin and Tom Robinson for sparing the time to read my manuscript and offering their helpful comments.

My grateful thanks are also due to Simon Heneage and Peter Bentley for giving me access to their collections and for allowing me to photograph material in their possession.

That my researches seldom became tedious was largely due to the friendly cooperation I received from the staff at the British Library, The National Library of Scotland, The National Newspaper Library and Reading University Library.

Among publishers I must thank Jonathan Cape, Constable, J. M. Dent, Hodder & Stoughton and Hutchinson for providing me with information from their archives, and Bell & Hyman and J. M. Dent for permission to reproduce illustrations for which they own the rights. I would also like to thank all those book-dealers who have allowed me to inspect their stock and make notes, often without making a purchase.

In writing this book I have made use of published material from many sources, the most important of which are listed in Appendix C to the Bibliography.

Finally, and most importantly, I must thank my wife Geraldine, for her constant encouragement and for her practical help in preparing the book for publication.

Preface

I first became aware of W. Heath Robinson's book illustrations in 1971 when on my honeymoon in the Lake District. Both my wife and I were already keen book collectors, and whilst searching through the stock in a small bookshop in Windermere we found and bought a copy of *Hans Andersen's Fairy Tales* with illustrations by Heath Robinson. From that time on I started to look for other books illustrated by him, and my next find was a copy of *Twelfth Night* with forty coloured plates. Visiting my local bookshop, I discovered *The Poems of Edgar Allen Poe* and *Uncle Lubin*, both of which had been issued in facsimile reprints. By the time that John Lewis's *Heath Robinson: Artist and Comic Genius* was published in 1973 I had become a dedicated collector. At first it seemed that this book would tell me all I needed to know, but as my own collection grew and I saw a wider range of material in catalogues and at bookfairs, I found myself asking more and more questions that it could not answer, and I started to keep detailed notes of all the books and magazines in which I had seen Heath Robinson's work.

An early and very exciting surprise came when my wife bought a large number of issues of *The Strand Magazine*. She had slowly been building up a collection of this magazine based on a run of the first twenty-two volumes that she had inherited from her great-grandfather, but up to that time had not extended it beyond 1911. With our new purchase came most of the issues for the period 1914 to 1916 and I saw for the first time the wonderful fairy tale illustrations that Heath Robinson had contributed to the magazine. Why, I wondered, had they been ignored in all of the books and articles written about Heath Robinson since that time? This led me to search for his work in other magazines. Lewis made a passing and rather disparaging mention of his illustrations for *Nash's Pall Mall Magazine*, but the quality of the one illustration he reproduced did not seem to justify this. I therefore went to the British Library to see for myself whether these drawings were mere hack work or, as I suspected, something of much greater worth. I was not disappointed. In fact the discovery was even more exciting than the finding of the fairy tale pictures in *The Strand Magazine*, for here was a large body of very fine serious illustrations executed at a time when, according to his biographers, he had virtually given up such work. Since that time I have found other equally fine examples of his illustrations in a variety of magazines, ranging from *The Quiver* to *Good Housekeeping*.

Whilst my major finds of unrecorded illustrations by Heath Robinson had been in magazines, I was also coming across a number of books containing his work that were not mentioned in any of the books or articles about the artist that I had read. More annoying than errors of omission, which are inevitable with such a prolific artist, were inaccuracies, including the attribution of books to wrong authors or to wrong publishers, wrongly identified first editions and the invention of non-existent reprints. These problems led me to think about compiling my own bibliography of the artist's work.

However, it was probably another factor that prompted me to undertake the large amount of work involved in realizing my idea. As a collector of Heath Robinson's work my main interest has always been in his illustrations rather than his cartoons. In my early days as a collector I concentrated exclusively on the illustrations, although more recently I have become less single-minded. I was therefore not pleased to find that when visiting bookshops, to mention what I was looking for generally led to my being directed to the 'humour' shelves. Similarly I found that to mention my interest to friends or colleagues would bring a silly grin to their faces accompanied by some comment about gadgets or contraptions. It was as if the reputation that grew up around Heath Robinson as 'The Gadget King' formed a barrier that hid his earlier achievements from the view of the general public. Even those few who were familiar with the lavish gift books that he illustrated between 1908 and 1921 seemed unaware that he had done any worthwhile work before that time. This prompted me to write a short article called 'Heath Robinson: The Early Illustrations' which was published in *Antiquarian Book Monthly Review* in September 1981. The article was well received, although looking back I can see that the accompanying bibliographical notes perpetuated as many errors as they corrected. From that seed the present volume grew.

I hope that this book will go some way towards restoring the balance in the general perception of Heath Robinson's standing as an artist by providing a comprehensive assessment of his activities in the fields of book and magazine illustration to stand alongside his already well known achievements as a humorist. I also hope that this book will make it easier for other collectors to seek out his work and make their own judgements based on as wide a range of material as possible.

Introduction

When Geoffrey Beare asked me to write an introduction to this book I was flattered but a little hesitant. His diligent researches have uncovered far more than I knew, particularly about my father's early professional career. What I can contribute, perhaps, is a reflection on the kind of man Will Heath Robinson was, as one of his children remembers him.

He was kindly, stern on rare occasions, never remote with those he knew; although he could be somewhat shy among strangers. Not a Victorian in the strict sense, he nevertheless expected children to observe simple courtesies. Our parents liked to be addressed formally as "mother" and "father", for example. I remember, too, that children's comics were not encouraged. Not, I think, on artistic grounds but because they were considered to be a little less edifying than say *The Boys' Own Paper* or *The Children's Newspaper*.

My father was happily at home with all children: his own five, his seventeen nieces and nephews and any others he came to know. Solemn nonsense was seldom far away. A cousin of mine recalls an occasion when my sister, very young at the time, invited two friends to tea. They found my father sitting in the dining-room with a flower-pot on his head. He looked so serious, the little girls dared not say a word, and tea proceeded with the flower-pot in place.

My father's fertile imagination flowered in the tales he told us when we were young, in the improbable friends he claimed to have known, in the 'useful' gadgets he conjured up. Of the last, I remember for no particular reason the perimanicula, designed — among other purposes — to remove gravy stains from gravel paths. My mother seemed to accept all this as a matter of course, although I doubt whether she was always quite sure in which generation to place Will. Luckily she was a composed and practical person. The eldest of five children and the only girl, and a product of the North London Collegiate School during the enlightened rule of the famous Miss Buss, she managed her own family cheerfully and without fuss.

My father's diversions, as I remember them (mainly from the ten years or so we lived at Cranleigh), were simple: working in the garden, the occasional trip to town and, of course, sketching the scenes that caught his eye in the surrounding countryside. He never possessed a motor-car (although he was more than willing to sit down and design one). He used his rather stately Humber bicycle for local travel, on occasion ferrying one or other of us on the step. For longer journeys there was always Mr. Belchamber who ran the garage in the village.

Sport held little interest for my father; nor was he much of a handyman about the house, disappointing though this must have been to critics of his day who saw in his cartoons all the signs of a frustrated engineer. At week-end gatherings, when songs at the piano were the order of the day, his favourite was 'The Farmer's Boy', sung with feeling in his pleasant baritone voice.

My father was a prodigious worker. This was inevitable with his particular style of draughtsmanship. But he could always find time to discuss and help us with our youthful interests. My own from my teens onward was in printing (and it has stayed with me all my life). To foster my enthusiasm he bought an ancient press which the local printer had no further use for, and which we succeeded in operating after various 'Heath Robinson' modifications.

When his work was over for the day and he was free to relax, he would settle down with a modest scotch, fill his pipe and pick up the book he was currently reading. It might be Plutarch's *Lives*, Samuel Pepys, T. E. Lawrence, or his favourite Dickens novel. He was widely travelled in his mind, if not in fact. Indeed, the only time he left these shores was when, as an artist correspondent for an American newspaper syndicate, he went to France in 1918 to depict the more light-hearted aspect of American troops at war and narrowly escaped being arrested as a spy.

My father was fortunate in that his career began at a time when technical innovations had paved the way to an upsurge in popularity of handsomely illustrated gift books. His work, and that of many notable contemporaries, was much in demand. But his sense of humour, as the reproductions in this book show, rarely emerged in his earlier work except in some of his illustrations to fairy tales, and in the two children's books he wrote and illustrated himself. In fact it was not very evident to publishers at the time, it would seem. There is a passage in his autobiography where he describes an interview with one eminent publisher to whom he had submitted some examples of his humorous work. After thoughtful consideration the great man pronounced judgment: 'if this is your humorous work, Mr. Robinson, your serious work must be very serious indeed'.

Our own familiarity, as children, with the more serious work was based on pictures on the walls at home and on cherished copies of the books. By the time we were old enough to take an interest in work in hand it was usually to see how the latest piece of machinery was getting on — and to offer free advice. This was politely received, if not acted upon.

By then the knotted string, cog wheels, candles and coal scuttles had to a large extent taken over, and it was as a comic genius — the gadget king — that Heath Robinson had become known. Fame meant nothing to him except at one stage. That was when it was widely put about that he was kept under restraint most of the time but, as a concession, allowed out once a week to sell his drawings. That, he felt, was really going too far. And yet, that flower-pot hat?

Nevertheless, it is only right to put on record that my father's qualities as an artist and his professional distinction did not depend on his mastery of the absurd alone. Romance, drama, the picturesque and the serene were as much within his grasp. That is what Geoffrey Beare has painstakingly sought to do.

OLIVER ROBINSON

Sources of Uncaptioned Pictures

Front Endpaper: Illustration from 'The Witch Girl', *Nash's Pall Mall Magazine*, 1929.

Title Page: Tailpiece from *The Giant Crab and Other Tales from Old India* (David Nutt, 1897).

Contents Page: Original design for *A Midsummer Night's Dream* (Constable & Co. Ltd., 1914).

Pp. 33, 85, 108: Tailpiece from *The Talking Thrush* (J. M. Dent & Co., 1899).

Rear Endpaper: Illustration from 'I'll Tell You Everything', *Nash's Pall Mall Magazine*, 1932.

1

The Formative Years

William Heath Robinson was born in the borough of Islington, North London, on the 31st May 1872. He had two older brothers and was to have two sisters and a brother younger than himself. The names William Heath were those of his maternal grandfather, but his talents as an illustrator must have come from his father's family who for two generations had been artists and craftsmen. His paternal grandfather had trained as a bookbinder in Newcastle-upon-Tyne and had worked for Thomas Bewick among others before travelling south to London where he gave up bookbinding in favour of wood engraving, working for such artists as John Gilbert, George Du Maurier and Fred Walker. William's father, Thomas, started his working life as a watch maker before moving on first to wood engraving and then to illustration, spending his later years as news illustrator for the *Penny Illustrated Paper*.

In his autobiography William describes his early years at some length and the picture he paints is of a happy and relaxed childhood in which the companionship of his older brothers Tom and Charles was an important element. Among other things he tells how, on a Sunday, the children would keenly watch the progress of their father's drawing for the next issue of the *Penny Illustrated Paper*, or 'Pip' as it was known, and it was at such times that the brothers received their first informal drawing lessons. He also describes how much of his amusement as a child came from the books that he and his brothers read, many of which were bought from secondhand booksellers of Holywell Street where he would have become familiar with the steel engraved illustrations of H.K. Browne and George Cruikshank as well as the woodcuts of the Sixties school.

Heath Robinson's formal training as an artist began at a small art school in North London and was continued at the Royal Academy Schools. He complained that at both an inordinate amount of time was spent in drawing from the antique, which perhaps accounts for the fact that in his early work many of the faces display the long straight nose and short upper lip so often seen in classical sculpture. Whilst this training was not particularly inspiring, neither was the young artist subjected to any strong influence within the schools, and he received a sound technical grounding.

On leaving art school his first inclination was towards landscape painting and it remained his first love throughout his life, but economic realities soon forced him to turn to a more readily saleable art form. In a chapter of his autobiography* entitled 'Bread and Butter' he tells how he was of necessity, but not unwillingly, drawn into the field of book illustration and how he started work in a small room off his father's studio. His brothers Tom and Charles had already embarked on careers in the same field and so it was natural that he should have followed them. At the end of 1895 Charles had just designed and illustrated a delightful edition of R. L. Stevenson's *A Child's Garden of Verses* for John Lane, which was very well received and was to be reprinted innumerable times through the years. He had also been accorded the honour of being discovered by *The Studio* magazine which had published an article devoted to his work, comparing him to such fashionable artists as Aubrey Beardsley and Charles Ricketts. He was therefore a young man in demand with publishers and must have had a strong influence on his younger brother as he started his career.

William got off to a slower start than Charles and his first attempts to obtain commissions from the London publishers met with little success. He got praise for his portfolio of drawings, but no firm offers of work until Cassell & Co. asked him to make two drawings for *Little Folks* magazine in 1896. The first of these, 'The Fairy Pedlar', confirms the influence of his brother Charles. The second is an illustration to the nursery rhyme 'Bo Peep' and in it he made good use of the single block of colour that was available to illustrators in *Little Folks* at that time.

Further magazine work came from Isbister & Co. who commissioned over fifty line drawings and a full page half-tone illustration to accompany a serial in *The Sunday Magazine*. This magazine had been a regular patron of the Sixties illustrators such as Du Maurier and these rather uninspired drawings are very much in that style. Ibster also asked for three drawings to illustrate a children's story by W. H. Hudson which was to appear in the same magazine and these alone give some hint of what was to follow. It should be noted that in his autobiography Heath Robinson confused *The Sunday Magazine* with *Good Words* for which he never worked, an error perpetuated by later biographers.

In 1897 the young artist must have been greatly encouraged by a commission from Bliss, Sands & Co. to illustrate three books for them, even though two of the three were to be part of a series of standard works which bore the legend 'The Cheapest Books in the World'. These were *The Pilgrim's Progress* and *Don Quixote*. They were printed on cheap paper which today usually appears brittle and brown at the edges,

* *My Line of Life* by W. Heath Robinson, Blackie & Son Ltd., 1938.

'... and the wind blew keen and cutting into the wanderer's face.'
Danish Fairy Tales and Legends (Bliss, Sands & Co., 1897)

although fortunately the illustrations were printed separately on heavily coated art paper. They were issued in lightweight red ribbed cloth bindings with roughly trimmed edges at 2s each, and although fairly common, are today difficult to find in good condition. The *Don Quixote* seems to have been the more popular of the two titles, having been reprinted at least four times and appearing in a variety of bindings. The drawings for these books are immature and show a lack of confidence, but already some of the qualities of his later work can be discerned. These include the use of novel viewpoints, often taking the reader very close to the scene that is depicted, and the use of strongly drawn foreground figures against a lightly sketched background to give depth to the illustrations. Occasionally, telling use is made of a small area of solid black in what is otherwise a purely line drawing, a device that was to be characteristic of the work of his brothers Charles and Tom.

The third book that Heath Robinson illustrated for Bliss, Sands & Co. in 1897 was *Danish Fairy Tales and Legends*, a collection of forty-five stories from Hans Andersen's *Eventyr* translated from the Danish by Mrs. Howitt. This volume was less austere in appearance than the other two, being bound in morocco grained cloth decorated with illustrations from the book blocked in gilt on the front and spine. The top edge was gilded and the quality of the paper slightly better, the whole being aimed at the lucrative school prize market. The price was 2s 6d. The drawings show greater confidence and a firmer line, and the last in the book is particularly striking, with the curving form of the windblown wanderer, reminiscent of Housman's wood engravings, set against the solid black sky which fills the top of the picture.

Heath Robinson went on to illustrate other books for this publisher, who by 1898 had dropped Mr. Bliss and become merely Sands & Co. One of these was an edition of Lamb's *Tales from Shakespeare* which was issued in a uniform format with the Andersen stories. It is not clear when the drawings for this book were executed, or precisely when it was first published, since the first edition is undated. The British Library copy of the book bears the date stamp 1902, but it seems likely that the drawings were contemporary with those for the earlier Bliss, Sands books. The artist was obviously not in sympathy with his subject, and these rather coarse and hurried drawings bear no relation to the fine illustrations that he was to produce in later years to two of Shakespeare's plays.

By the mid-1900s Sands & Co. had gone out of business and some time later a publisher called Alexander Gardner of Paisley near Glasgow in Scotland brought out reprints of *Pilgrim's Progress* and *Danish Fairy Tales and Legends*, followed in 1909 by *Tales from Shakespeare*. These are chiefly of interest because for this printing the two children's books had coloured frontispieces, for which in each case a different illustration from the one in the Sands & Co. edition was used, the pictures chosen being more suitable for reproduction with added colour. The Andersen seems to have been issued in haste since the list of plates was not amended to reflect these changes.

Heath Robinson's next book was *The Giant Crab*, a collection of Indian folk tales retold by W. H. D. Rouse. This was published by David Nutt and was issued in time to appear in his Christmas list for 1897. In this list Heath Robinson found himself in good company, for his new book appeared alongside the books of fairy tales collected by Joseph Jacobs and illustrated by John Batten, Judge Parry's *Katawampus* illustrated by Archie MacGregor and Oscar Wilde's *Happy Prince* illustrated by Walter Crane. In this book he was presented with a subject that allowed him to give free rein to his imagination and was no longer constrained to a series of full page plates, the whole book being printed on good quality paper. As a result he produced a highly original set of drawings which display an increased self-confidence and freedom of interpretation as well as on occasions a great sense of fun and mischief. The obvious sympathy between artist and subject is matched by the way the best of the drawings intertwine with the text. In two of the drawings he makes use of the circular frame that was to reappear in many of his books over the years, whilst in the cover design one can see the first influence of the art nouveau style that was becoming fashionable. It is therefore not surprising that two years later he was asked to provide a similar set of drawings for a second collection of Indian tales by Rouse called *The Talking Thrush*, this time published by Dent.

In 1898 he illustrated his first book for Constable & Co., a publisher with whom he was to enjoy a long and fruitful association. This was *The Queen's Story Book*, another contender for the school prize market and one of a series of four books edited by Laurence Gomme telling stories from English history associated with kings, queens, princes and princesses respectively. It was a handsomely produced volume in dark blue cloth, brightly blocked in gilt with stylized images of queens, crowns and a lion, but inside the artist was once more limited to full page line drawings reproduced on heavily coated art paper and thus separated from the text. The result was a set of drawings similar to those for the Bliss, Sands books, although in one or two of the more successful illustrations he started to explore the possibilities of predominantly dark scenes, a theme he was to develop the following year.

During 1898 Heath Robinson received two commissions from Cassell & Co. to illustrate children's stories for *The Quiver* magazine. The first of these is of little interest, but the second, a fairy parable by Roma White

' "Who are you lady?" it asked her.'
Illustration from 'The Birth of the Crocus',
The Quiver, 1898

called 'The Birth of the Crocus' inspired three drawings that must rank with the best that he had produced to date, displaying control of line and a developing sense of the decorative possibilities of his subject.

Towards the end of the year he was again working for Constable, this time as one of five artists used to illustrate an edition of *The Arabian Nights* which was to be issued in twenty weekly parts. He was commissioned to produce 250 drawings, with at least three full page illustrations in every thirty, to be delivered at the rate of thirty per month. He was to be paid 15s for each drawing as long as the rate of delivery was maintained. In the event he contributed something over two hundred drawings out of a total of five hundred and fifty, as well as the wrapper design. Not surprisingly, some of the drawings show signs of haste, but the project presented a wonderful opportunity to experiment, both with the content and format of the illustrations. It was one that he accepted wholeheartedly, making use of large areas of black or unbroken expanses of white in the compositions and adopting unusual viewpoints from which to depict the chosen scenes. If some of the drawings look back to *The Giant Crab* for their inspiration, others look forward to the drawings he was to make for

'We've sent our little cupids ashore.' Frontispiece for *The Collected Verse
of Rudyard Kipling* (Doubleday, Page & Co., New York, 1910)

Four editions of
The Adventures of Uncle Lubin,
1902, 1925, (*and below*), 1972, 1975

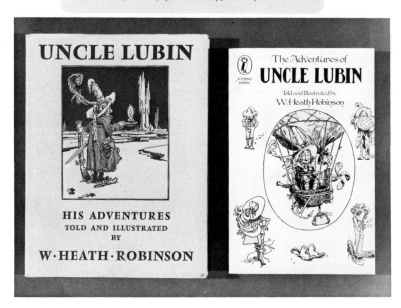

The Poems of Edgar Allen Poe and *Rabelais*. The work was published in book form by George Newnes in 1899 in a handsome pictorial binding with decorations based on Heath Robinson's drawings and with all edges gilded. A number of the drawings were reused in later years by Constable and others for different editions of the *Arabian Nights* stories, but these were all inferior to the original.

In September 1899 Dent published a new edition of *Andersen's Fairy Tales*, using a new translation of the stories by Mrs. E. Lucas, for which they commissioned drawings from all three Robinson brothers. Frank Swinnerton, who worked in Dent's outer office at the time, remembered their visits. He wrote:

> They used to swing into the Dent shop at 29-30 Bedford St. like the three musketeers. My memory is of Tom, rather small and sedate, first; Will, very thin and taller than the others, in an overcoat which was so closely buttoned that he looked thinner than ever, in the middle; and Charles, always freer and more jaunty in his movements than the others, last.
>
> They would stand talking with me while they waited until Mr. Dent could see them, and then they filed upstairs. What happened then I don't know; but soon afterwards they would come clattering down again like schoolboys, always very much amused at what had happened above.

The new edition of Andersen was issued in an extremely attractive pictorial binding by Charles which sadly, because of the shape of the book and the quality of the cloth, is now usually found in less than perfect condition. Each of the brothers contributed between thirty and forty drawings and the high spots are William's although he was the youngest of the three. His use of predominantly dark illustrations for this book may have been inspired by H.K. Browne's dark plates for Dickens and Ainsworth with which he must have been familiar, and the substantial reduction of these drawings on the printed page gives a texture similar to steel engravings to some of them. Another possible inspiration was S.H. Sime who at that time used dark backgrounds for many of his drawings; the picture of the little match girl in the snow would not look out of place amongst that artist's work. Whatever the source of the experiment, it led to a number of highly original and appropriate drawings that emphasise the sombre side of Andersen's writing. Unfortunately the high standard achieved in most of them was not maintained throughout. The introductory drawing to 'The Snow Queen' is hideous, making the queen look like some ageing fertility goddess.

The book was obviously a great success and by 1939 had been

'Remember that I impatiently await your return.'
The Arabian Nights Entertainments (George Newnes Ltd., 1899)

'She took off her red shoes, her most
cherished possessions, and threw them in the river.'
Fairy Tales From Hans Christian Andersen
(J. M. Dent & Co., 1899)

reprinted as many as fourteen times.
Dent also made use of some of the
illustrations in other editions of
Andersen's Fairy Tales that they published. These included a pocket
edition in their 'Temple Classics for
Young People' series in 1901. *Dent's
Andersen in German* in 1902 and the
Everyman edition, which was first
published in 1906, and which was to
remain in print until 1960. In the
original edition the story of 'The
Ugly Duckling' was not illustrated,
but in the Temple Classics edition
the story has one full page illustration by Heath Robinson, whilst
in the version in German it has three,
the one from the Temple Classics
edition, one previously unpublished
and one borrowed from the story of
'The Marsh King's Daughter'.

Towards the end of 1899 Heath
Robinson submitted to George Bell
& Sons some specimen drawings he
had prepared for an illustrated edition of Lord Byron's epic poem
'Childe Harold'. Although im-
pressed by the drawings the publishers did not think the text a suitable
one and asked him to suggest a
similar but smaller work. He wrote
in reply:

'A poor little girl was wandering
in the dark cold streets.'
*Fairy Tales from Hans Christian
Andersen* (J. M. Dent & Co., 1899)

> ... may I suggest an *Ingoldsby
> Legends*. I think my style would
> suit this and I should delight in
> illustrating it. *Don Quixote* too I should very much like to illustrate.
>
> I do not remember to have seen an illustrated edition of Poe's poems,
> this particularly would give me immense scope.

It is indicative of both his powers of self criticism and his increased self
confidence that he should want to illustrate *Don Quixote* again only three
years after the publication of the Bliss, Sands edition. However it was his
suggestion of Poe's poems that appealed to Bell, who had recently started

Illustration from 'Ulalume'
The Poems of Edgar Allen Poe
(George Bell & Sons, 1900)

to publish illustrated volumes of poetry in 'The Endymion Series'. On 2nd January 1900 Heath Robinson visited Edward Bell and agreed to do seventy drawings to illustrate *The Poems of Edgar Allen Poe* for £50, an auspicious start to the new century. The drawings were delivered by midsummer and in September Bell had printed four thousand copies of a prospectus for the book. This consisted of four pages printed in red and black and included sample illustrations. In October a thousand copies of the book were published at 6s each, and there was also a limited edition of 75 copies printed on Japanese vellum at a guinea. Although the final volume contained over one hundred illustrations Heath Robinson was paid only the £50 originally agreed. Sales of the book were initially depressed by the death of Queen Victoria on 22nd January 1901, but by the end of June that year Bell's stock was down to one hundred and one copies of the trade edition and forty one of the limited edition, and in September a second printing of a thousand copies was made. This second printing sold more slowly and in September 1907 new title pages were printed for the remaining three hundred and fifty sets of sheets from the 1901 printing. Bell must then have made some effort to promote the book, because in January 1909 a third printing of five hundred copies was made. As an economy measure this was issued in a binding originally designed by R. Anning Bell for the volume of Shelley's poems in the same series, which was now adopted for all the titles. This printing was sold at the reduced price of 3s 6d.

When the book was first published a reviewer in *The Studio* magazine wrote:

'But evil things, in robes of sorrow, Assailed the monarch's high estate...'

The Poems of Edgar Allen Poe (George Bell & Sons, 1900)

Illustration from 'Ulalume'
The Poems of Edgar Allen Poe (George Bell & Sons, 1900)

> Mr. Heath Robinson's numerous decorations and illustrations display
> much charm and delicacy of execution, and they proclaim him a most
> worthy disciple of the modern school of penmen.

This modern school had grown up when the newly developed zinc line
block replaced wood engraving as the primary means of reproducing black
and white illustrations. For the first time an artist could draw a picture on
paper or board and know that his image would be exactly reproduced on
the printed page. Furthermore, he could have his drawing reduced onto
the block, making the printed image finer than the original. The limitation
of the technique was that it could print only in black and white, with no
intermediate tones, and it was this limitation that was exploited by the
new school. They absorbed the lessons of simplification and stylization
embodied in the Japanese prints that had recently started to be published
in Europe, and following the lead of artists such as Beardsley and Whistler
established a new style of decorative illustration.

Earlier volumes in 'The Endymion Series' had been illustrated by Byam
Shaw, R. Anning Bell and A. Garth Jones, and Heath Robinson said that

he was gratified to be invited to join such a select company. Other artists of the new school whose influence he acknowledged included S. H. Sime, Walter Crane and his brother Charles. Another influence was the art nouveau style which had begun in Scotland and by the turn of the century had spread through book illustration, painting and domestic and commercial design, both in England and on the Continent. This had been reflected in a few of Heath Robinson's earlier drawings for books such as *The Arabian Nights*, but in the Poe drawings he embraces the style completely, not just as a follower of fashion, but adapting its sinuous outlines and rich textures to achieve a fine balance between illustration and decoration. In this book his experiments in composition and in the balancing of solid areas of black and white come to fruition, and in drawings such as those to 'The Bells' or 'The Haunted Palace' he had added to Beardsley's decorative values of line and contrast a feeling of rhythmical movement and grace.

Soon after the publication of *The Poems of E. A. Poe* Heath Robinson suggested to Edward Bell that he should illustrate a volume of Dante's poetry to be published in the same series, and in January 1901 he wrote:

> I have been reading the edition of Dante you lent me and needless to say feel all the more desirous of illustrating it. I learnt a lot in illustrating 'Poe's Poems' and feel that now I could do much better work of this kind. I think too that this work would lend itself more easily to decorative line drawing.

Sadly, Bell felt that the Dante would be too great an undertaking, although whether for artist or publisher is not clear. Perhaps the poor sales of the Poe poems at the time of Victoria's death weighed too heavily in the balance. Whatever the reason, the loss is ours, and the lessons that Heath Robinson had learnt in illustrating Poe were not to be fully realized for another twelve years.

With the exception of four drawings in *The Quiver* magazine, nothing new by Heath Robinson appears to have been published in 1901, although it is likely that one or more of the books bearing the date 1902 was in fact ready for the Christmas market that year. *Mediaeval Stories* was published by Sands & Co. and is a much better product than their earlier series of classics, having been printed at the University of Aberdeen Press on good quality paper. The uneven quality of the drawings and variety of styles indicate that once again the artist was not inspired by his text. Perhaps the most attractive of his contributions are the decorative head and tail pieces, and in these, as in the bold endpaper design, the art nouveau influence continued.

It was in 1902 that Heath Robinson got the chance he had been seeking to illustrate *Don Quixote* again, not from Bell but from J. M. Dent. His confidence in himself proved to be justified and the drawings for this book are a great improvement on the earlier Bliss, Sands edition, which was reprinted in competition. This time the illustrations are full of tension, often seeming to more than fill their frames and many give the impression of looking from a dark room onto the brightly sunlit Spanish scene outside. A few of them are reminiscent of the 1899 *Andersen's Fairy Tales* in their use of backlighting or in being dark scenes. Once again the artist shows a willingness to experiment with his medium by including seven drawings in chalk, and whilst they are not as effective as the sharper pen drawings they do add variety to the book. Also worthy of note are the decorative borders to the drawings, some of which are very elaborate, providing a humorous aside on the subject depicted.

In January 1902 Heath Robinson wrote once again to Edward Bell with an idea for a book. He was at this time sharing a studio with his old friend Percy Billingshurst who had recently illustrated books of fables by Aesop and La Fontaine for John Lane, and he wrote:

> Our idea is to illustrate together *Gay's Fables*. You will remember that these are not only of animals but many could be illustrated by figure subjects. We find that we could so arrange it as to have half the pictures of animal subjects by Mr. Billingshurst ... and the other half figure subjects by myself ... I am sure I could not have a better opportunity for my work than this book would afford.

Edward Bell did not take up the idea, and in fact was never to publish another book by Heath Robinson. However, if he had lost one publisher he soon found another who was to be very important to him over the next three years. This was that ebullient Edwardian character Grant Richards, who in 1902 published two books that were innovations for Heath Robinson; his first book illustrated in colour and the first book that he both wrote and illustrated. The former was a rather uninteresting reprint of *The Surprising Adventures of Baron Munchausen* with four poorly reproduced coloured plates. The latter was *The Adventures of Uncle Lubin*, 'that rare good thing for children' as H. G. Wells called it in one of his novels. The story is episodic in form, telling the tale of Uncle Lubin, a little old man in a tall hat and long coat, as he attempts to retrieve his nephew, Baby Peter, from the clutches of the wicked bag bird. The figure of Uncle Lubin had first appeared in *The Talking Thrush* three years earlier and was to reappear in 1906 in an illustration for *Little Folks* magazine, this time at the seaside with six children. In his autobiography Heath Robinson refers to Lubin as his 'strange little genius' that tempted him along a path that ran quite independently of his more serious work and

Posting himself in the midst of the highway.

Illustration from *The Adventures of Don Quixote of La Mancha*
(J. M. Dent & Co., 1902)

Illustration from *The Adventures of Uncle Lubin*
(Grant Richards, 1902)

on the dustwrapper of that book shows himself on the end of a piece of
knotted string being led by the strange little man in the tall hat.

It was not only his direction in art that was changed by *Uncle Lubin*,
for indirectly it provided the financial support that enabled Heath
Robinson to marry. A Canadian named Chas. Ed. Potter on reading the

book decided that this was the artist to illustrate some advertisements that he was writing for the Lamson Paragon Supply Co. Ltd., a task for which Heath Robinson was paid in cash as each drawing was delivered. So although *Uncle Lubin* was not a best seller, it was the means of gaining at least a degree of security for the young artist who was married to Josephine Latey, daughter of the editor of *The Penny Illustrated Paper*, in 1903.

Potter also commissioned Heath Robinson to design a bookplate. The result was a gloomy and pretentious neo-classical design showing a seated artist painting pots under a marble arch on which are balanced three more pots labelled commerce, art and literature!

The first edition of *Uncle Lubin* was completely designed by Heath Robinson from covers, through pictorial endpapers to the setting of the pages of text. Each of these starts with a large pictorial capital printed in red, with the words winding down past a related line drawing until by the bottom of the page they have in many cases diminished to a single column. Opposite each page of text is a full page line drawing, and these are full of invention. They are carefully executed without a wasted stroke of the pen. The figure of Uncle Lubin is expressively drawn and one can share his feeling of helplessness as the bag bird flies away with baby Peter, his sadness as he awakes from his dream or his sheer embarrassment at being embraced by the grateful Rajah.

In the book one can detect a number of ideas that were later to be developed either by himself or others. Uncle Lubin's dream introduces an image of the fairy world that was to be the starting point for a number of the pictures in *A Midsummer Night's Dream*, whilst the giant that Vammadopper met was only the first in a series of giants and ogres that Heath Robinson was to portray. Both the airship and submarine are met with time and again as the subjects of cartoons during the first world war and after. It seems likely that Uncle Lubin's escape from the flood, using his upturned umbrella as a boat, inspired the similar escape of Pooh bear many years later in the story of *Winnie the Pooh*.

Uncle Lubin was dedicated to his young niece Edith Mary Robinson, known to the family as Bay, who was the first child of his brother Charles. The first edition is now scarce and commands high prices, but fortunately the book was reprinted in a number of editions. The second, for which Heath Robinson produced a new full colour dust wrapper design, was published by Chatto & Windus in 1925 and, at the time of writing, an attractive paperback edition is still in print.

The following year saw the publication by Dent of *Rama and the Monkeys*, another book of Indian folk tales, this time adapted by Geraldine Hodgson from *The Ramayana*. The book, which had a chromo-

Illustration from *Rama and the Monkeys*
(J. M. Dent & Co., 1903)

lithographed frontispiece and title page and six line drawings, was published as one of the 'Temple Classics for Young People'. This was a well printed series of pocket sized books sold either in blue cloth at 1s 6d or in limp leather at 2s. Today the cloth bindings are much to be preferred as the spines of the leather bound volumes have usually rotted. Heath Robinson's eldest brother Tom was the most frequently used illustrator for the series, which also included *Perrault's Fairy Tales* illustrated by Charles and the first version of *Gulliver's Travels* to be illustrated by Arthur Rackham. All of these books are difficult to find and *Rama and the Monkeys* is one of the scarcest titles, but it is well worth searching for. The drawings show a freshness of approach in their composition and are well suited to the text. The portrait of Hanuman is given a decorative treatment, with the backlit figure of the leader of the monkeys seated on the edge of a pool that reflects his image. A slender tree rises on either side of the figure and each is balanced by a water lily floating on the pool. In the picture of Rama lifting the mystical bow of Janaka a three-dimensional effect is achieved by the thickening of the outline of the figure in the foreground.

In 1903 Heath Robinson continued to work for Grant Richards, writing and illustrating *The Child's Arabian Nights*. This is a much less attractive book than *Uncle Lubin* and was obviously aimed at very young children. It has twelve full page coloured plates which were chromolithographed in Nottingham by Thomas Storer, and a number of line drawings, all in a simple and somewhat crude style. The most attractive feature of the book is its front cover showing an old bearded arab's head surrounded by those of children, all wearing brightly coloured turbans. The same year Heath Robinson also produced four coloured plates in a similar style to be included in *Grant Richards' Children's Annual for 1904* which was issued in time for Christmas 1903.

His next book for Grant Richards could not have been more different, and was his largest and most ambitious project to date. This was *The Works of Rabelais* which was published in two large volumes containing a hundred full page illustrations and well over a hundred smaller drawings and vignettes. The project was almost certainly suggested to the publisher by Heath Robinson, and the text is the sort of loosely linked episodic

Illustration from *Rama and the Monkeys*
(J. M. Dent & Co., 1903)

narrative that appealed to him so much. The grotesque heads used as tail pieces throughout the book, which probably owe something to Leonardo da Vinci, are most striking when seen grouped on a single page as in the studies that he prepared for the book, one of which was reproduced in *The Strand Magazine*. However, it is the full page drawings that are the most original, with visions of hell that are truly horrific, and a raw power and earthiness in the drawings that is exactly in tune with Rabelais' narrative style. These drawings must have influenced illustrators who followed and many of them bring to mind the work of Mervyn Peake forty years later.

The costs involved in printing this extravagant edition of Rabelais' works contributed to the failure of the publishing house of Grant Richards

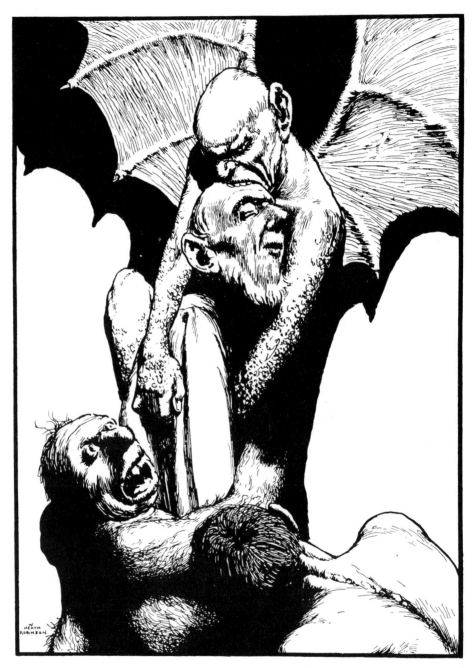

'O the terrible Coyl that they keep!'
The Works of Rabelais (Grant Richards, 1904)

which was announced in November 1904. After protracted negotiations the stocks and copyrights were sold to Alexander Moring Ltd.; of the De La More press, enabling a dividend of two shillings in the pound to be paid to creditors, one of whom was Heath Robinson. He thus received little financial reward for all the work he had done for this publisher. Under the circumstances the book was not a great success when first published, but was reprinted in reduced formats many times in later years. A.E.Johnson writing in 1913 seemed to prefer the more convenient format of the reduced edition published by Alexander Moring that year, but the price of convenience is too high. The fine gravure frontispieces of the first edition are replaced by poor half tone plates, a number of the smaller drawings and vignettes are omitted, and both the pictorial endpapers and the binding design are also lost.

The other book that Heath Robinson illustrated in 1904 was memorable for its title rather than its illustrations. This was *The Merry Multifleet and the Mounting Multicorps* by Thomas O'Cluny, a tale of a marvellous invention that could multiply the image of an object to which it was applied whether this was a suit of armour on horseback or a warship. In later years Heath Robinson would have made much of such a subject, but in this case the illustrations have nothing to recommend them and are barely recognisable as his work.

In 1905 the first of Heath Robinson's cartoons were published in *The Tatler*, *The Sketch* and *The Bystander*. These were all executed in pen and wash heightened in white and were reproduced by the half-tone process. It was probably the appearance of these pictures that prompted *Pall Mall Magazine* to commission him to illustrate a children's story by Edith Nesbit for their Christmas number of that year. The story, entitled 'Septimus Septimusson', was a good one and Heath Robinson produced a fitting and somewhat eccentric set of drawings for it. These were executed in pen and wash and each has a pictorial border in line which, as with the *Don Quixote* drawings, provides a humorous comment on the subject of the main picture. The first illustration showing young Septimus standing on a beach talking to the mussels makes effective use of a low viewpoint and an unusual shape, filling the full height of the page, but only half of the width. It is interesting to compare Heath Robinson's illustrations for this story with the far more traditional line drawings by Arthur Rackham for another fairy story in the same issue.

During 1905 Heath Robinson was asked by the firm of T.C. & E.C. Jack to make a series of eight coloured illustrations for an edition of Chaucer's stories in their new 'Told to Children' series. This, as the name implies, was a series of books of selected stories from the classics retold in simple language for young people. The books were issued in small

format either in cloth gilt at 1s 6d or in paper covered boards at 1s, each binding having one of the illustrations repeated on the front cover. Whilst some of the compositions are interesting, it is obvious that he was still feeling his way as an illustrator in colour, and the result is a competent but uninspired set of pictures. However, the publishers seem to have been well pleased, and later the same year asked Heath Robinson to illustrate two more books in the same series, *The Iliad* and *The Odyssey*. These also had eight plates each and the majority of them are very ordinary, only one or two rising a little above the general level of mediocrity.

The same year J. M. Dent published a children's annual, *The Children's Christmas Treasury of Things New and Old*, a beautifully produced book in a multi-coloured cloth binding by Reginald Knowles. Inside the stories and poems were illustrated by Arthur Rackham, Alice Woodward, R. Anning Bell, Patten Wilson, the three

'"I know I'm a coward," said Sep.'
Illustration to 'Septimus Septimusson',
Pall Mall Magazine, 1905

26

Robinson brothers and others, in both colour and black and white. The 'new' contributions by Heath Robinson were illustrations in red and black to a story by E. V. Lucas called 'The Monkey's Revenge' and a double-page cartoon in full colour. The 'old' ones included the full page illustration to 'The Monkey's Rebuke', a story taken from *The Talking Thrush* published by Dent in 1899. This was partly coloured in red and has Heath Robinson's initials added in red, which indicates that he was responsible for the colouring. One of the high spots in the book is the full page illustration to 'Hans Clodhopper' by Heath Robinson, taken from Dent's 1899 *Andersen's Fairy Tales* which has been fully coloured, and which on the larger page size of the book makes an extremely handsome picture. The book is now quite scarce, perhaps having been too expensive to achieve the larger sales it deserved, and because of its interest to Rackham collectors can command very high prices.

The following year the Caxton Publishing Co. produced a cheap set of Thackeray's works that included *Barry Lyndon* and *Men's Wives* in one volume with six illustrations by Heath Robinson. Three of these are coloured and the other three are line drawings printed in sepia, and there is also a gravure frontispiece by Gordon Browne. When these drawings were made and under what circumstances is not clear, since in style they are closer to the Bliss, Sands books than anything published later. The coloured plates are tinted line drawings and may have been coloured some time after they were first drawn. The effect is reminiscent of the hand coloured engravings of a hundred years earlier and this is perhaps what was intended.

In 1906 Heath Robinson was again asked to illustrate a children's story for the Christmas issue of *Pall Mall Magazine*, 'The Peach Stone' by W. H. Bryce-Stacpoole. As for the previous year, the illustrations were drawn in pen and wash heightened with white and are similar in style. The story had an Arabian setting and the one full page drawing entitled 'The Caliphe of All the Children in Bagdad' (*sic*) is a development from the cover design to *The Child's Arabian Nights*. These illustrations are in sharp contrast to the whimsical line drawings that he made for the first special Christmas number of *Little Folks* magazine the same year.

For *Pearson's Magazine* he was asked to illustrate a cricketing story by an up and coming young writer called P. G. Wodehouse. Heath Robinson never claimed any great success at sports, but he did recall one great triumph on the cricket field when he was nine years old. He had by some chance been made vice captain of his school eleven, and remembering the occasion in his autobiography he wrote:

... I was put on to bowl. I think I must have been a last hope. We had been trying for the whole afternoon to end the innings of a local Bradman.

My over-arm bowling was never my strong point. The ball was liable to take an erratic and dangerous course; so I tried some skilful underhand work. I sent the ball slowly along the wicket; it was hardly in the air for one moment. With what eagerness I watched that ball as it rolled gently through the grass! it crawled past the batsman in spite of the vicious and misdirected swipe he made at it. It then touched a stump with only sufficient impact to dislodge one of the bails. I tried these tactics again and succeeded in taking four wickets in succession and saved the game for my side.

The story by Wodehouse was called 'The Pro' and in the headpiece for it Cupid is seen having the same devastating effect on the hero's wicket as Heath Robinson had had on those of his opponents.

Heath Robinson's next venture as an illustrator in colour was *The Monarchs of Merry England* and its sequel *More Monarchs of Merry England*. These two volumes together comprise a comic history of England from the Norman Conquest to contemporary times written in verse by Roland Carse and for them Heath Robinson made a total of forty large coloured illustrations and many small line drawings. The first volume containing the first two parts of the history was published by its printer, Alf Cooke Ltd., in 1907. The second volume, containing parts three and four, was published by T. Fisher Unwin the following year. These volumes were each issued in pictorial boards with designs on the front and back by Heath Robinson. The front of the first showed a bespectacled king in armour followed by his page and carrying a banner with the title of the book on it, whilst the front of the second had a picture of Charles I in full regalia with four spaniels each led by a red silk ribbon. A few copies of the book also exist with each of the four parts in a separate volume bound in titled boards with a trimmed coloured plate from that volume mounted on the front. The British Library copies are in this format and it therefore seems likely that this was a preliminary binding used only on advance copies. The books were reprinted by Alf Cooke some years later, also in four parts, but this time bound in pictorial card covers with only two coloured plates to each part.

Although a few of the illustrations are similar to the drawings for Rabelais, the majority are closer to the style of his cartoons for *The Sketch*. In fact in 1907 that magazine published a cartoon showing how Charles II escaped detection after the battle of Worcester by disguising himself as the upper half of a broken telegraph pole and this might equally well have been used in the book. One of the best of the illustrations shows a seedy looking Blondel, complete with howling mongrel, serenading an exasperated Richard I who is thrusting his head through a tiny window in the wall of the castle in which he is imprisoned. The composition is reminiscent of the illustration to *Rama and the Monkeys* that shows Ravana leaning from the window of his tower and glaring at the army of monkeys below.

In the opening years of the century publishers had started to produce sumptuous editions of books with coloured illustrations printed by the new three colour process. These illustrations had to be printed on heavily coated art paper which was unsuited to the printing of text and liable to crack if folded, and so they were printed on single pages and tipped in to the book. This method was first used for travel books such as A & C Black's series of colour books, but was not entirely satisfactory as the illustrations were liable to come loose as the pages were turned. A more permanent way of inserting the coloured illustrations, used for *de luxe* editions, was to stick or tip a trimmed illustration onto a card which could then be sewn in, and these mounts were often made a decorative feature of the book. Soon a wide range of gift books in this format were being published, aimed at both adults and children. In 1905 Heinemann published *Rip Van Winkle* with fifty coloured plates by Arthur Rackham and Hodder & Stoughton entered the market in 1907 with *The Arabian Nights* illustrated by Edmund Dulac, also with fifty tipped in plates. These books sold well and publishers were looking both for texts suited to the new gift book format and for artists to illustrate them. Hodder & Stoughton started to issue a series of Shakespeare's plays each with forty coloured plates, the first of which were *The Tempest* illustrated by Dulac and *Twelfth Night* by Heath Robinson. They were published in November 1908 priced at 10s 6d for the trade edition or 42s for the limited edition, and the following month *The Bookman* special Christmas number included a portfolio of plates from the two books.

In his illustrations to *Twelfth Night* Heath Robinson did not attempt to provide a literal record of the action, but rather to convey its atmosphere, approaching his task rather as a composer might set about writing incidental music. The illustrations therefore do not relate evenly to the text, but concentrate on those passages that appealed to him, and in particular on the songs, which provide more than a quarter of the subjects. Although free from the limitation of a stage setting, many of the illustrations retain a theatrical atmosphere and the high viewpoints chosen for some of them give one the feeling of looking down from a box or the upper circle in an old fashioned theatre. Once again Heath Robinson was experimenting, this time with the effects of light. It is seen filtering through trees or buildings to dapple the ground beneath, reflected from puddles and fountains, or diffused by the early morning mist. Tones vary from the warmth of a Turner sunset to the cold of a moonlit night. In the illustrations one can see a variety of styles, and he was still searching for one of his own. The picture entitled 'What country, friends, is this?' reminds one of Dulac's work, whilst that to 'My name is Mary, sir,' which was also used for the pictorial dustwrapper to the book, could easily be the work of Hugh Thomson. He comes closest to what was to be his own style in illustrations to the songs, such as the clown singing 'The rain it raineth every day' or the dancing circle of woodland numphs illustrating 'Present mirth hath present laughter'.

A. E. Johnson says that the pictures were completed in urgent haste and this accounts for the poor finish of some of them in which a carefully executed foreground figure is seen against a hastily daubed background. However, in other illustrations full advantage is taken of the decorative qualities of the finely drawn architectural backgrounds, demonstrating yet another facet of Heath Robinson's technical skill as an artist.

The watercolours for the book were exhibited in 1908 and the show was acclaimed a 'triumphant success'. *The Westminster Gazette* said that

> Mr. Robinson must be accepted henceforth as a watercolour painter of high rank, with a very valuable and refreshing gift of originality and poetry.

The publishers were delighted with the work and in their advertisements for the book Hodder & Stoughton promised that the public had

> ...a rare pleasure to look forward to, for these forty paintings are all admirably reproduced in full colour in a volume which, at half a guinea, is admittedly one of the marvels of publishing.

Mr. J. E. Hodder Williams personally wrote to Heath Robinson:

> I want to send you my very hearty congratulations upon the completion of your great work... I think the work is wonderful, and I have every hope that it will be a great success... I am going to ask you as a special favour to let me have one or two original sketches for my own specially done up copy of the Edition de Luxe. I want to keep a memento of the production of a work of which I am immensely proud, and a permanent reminder of a business transaction which has been from the first the greatest possible pleasure...

Heath Robinson obliged by adding a drawing to Mr. Hodder Williams copy of the book and by giving him one of the original watercolours.

The success of *Twelfth Night* resulted in an immediate commission for another book from Hodder & Stoughton. This was *A Song of the English*, a poem by Rudyard Kipling taken from *The Seven Seas*, and a contract was signed on 9th December 1908, only a few days after *Twelfth Night* first appeared in the shops. The publishers agreed to pay £250 for thirty coloured plates plus £1 11s 6d for each black and white drawing 'which the publishers may consider it wise to include.' The pictures were to be delivered by 30th June, 1909, and Mr. A.E. Johnson was called upon to 'use his utmost endeavours to secure their exhibition in some public gallery.'

The commission was a formidable one. A single poem, which in the original book took up only seventeen pages, was here stretched to over a hundred, and in these short verses Heath Robinson had to find subjects for thirty coloured plates and twice as many line drawings. He started by visiting the author to discuss the book and he later commented on Kipling's sympathetic understanding of his role in the project, describing his day at the author's Sussex home as both happy and helpful. He must have started to look about him for inspiration and one place that he found it was in the volume of *Coleridge's Poems* illustrated by Gerald Metcalfe that had been published by John Lane in 1907. Metcalfe, a contemporary of Heath Robinson, was primarily a portrait artist and miniaturist, but his line drawings for Coleridge's Poems, especially those to 'The Ancient Mariner', show him to have been capable of producing imaginatively expressive and decorative book illustrations. One of them shows a sailing ship seen from beneath the surface of the water, a device adopted by Heath Robinson for his coloured illustration entitled 'The Wrecks that dissolve above us'. Metcalfe's influence can also be traced in the black and white drawings with their strongly emphasized pen strokes and flowing lines.

Whilst there are a number of impressive illustrations in the book, many of them are not easily accessible to the modern reader. To appreciate them one must adjust to an Edwardian sense of pride in Empire together with an unashamed love of the sentimental that made a book such as *A Song of the English* not just acceptable but extremely popular. Illustrations such as 'When the last water dried' show that the Victorian taste for narrative painting had survived into the new century.

A.E. Johnson succeeded in organizing an exhibition of both the watercolours and the drawings for the book at the Baillie Galleries in October 1909. The reviewer in *The Studio* magazine praised the drawings, but thought the coloured illustrations less successful. He concluded by saying that although Heath Robinson was

> …always an artist of much imagination and invention, perhaps allegory of this kind has not afforded him the happiest opportunity for his lively and resourceful art.

However, two months later another critic reviewing the book for the same magazine wrote:

> Mr. Heath Robinson has, by sheer merit, gained for himself a prominent position amongst English illustrators of the day, and he has in this branch of art produced nothing finer than the series of coloured and pen-and-ink drawings for Kipling's *Song of the English*

The variety of published editions of the book and the span of time over which they were issued testify to its popularity.

His success with *A Song of the English* led to two more commissions to illustrate Kipling. The first was from Doubleday, Page & Co. in New York and was for nine coloured plates and a number of line drawings to illustrate the American edition of *The Collected Verse of Rudyard Kipling*. Again the artist does not seem to be entirely happy with his text. Whereas with *A Song of the English* it was difficult to find enough subjects within the limited scope of the poem, in this case it was the very diversity of the poems that was the problem, making it difficult to define a single atmosphere or common feeling that could unify the illustrations. He is at his best with the comic-macabre coloured illustration to the poem 'Tomlinson', which owes much to the painting of S. H. Sime, whilst of the remainder it is the line drawings that are the most successful. The book was not published in England, presumably for reasons of copyright, but was available in Canada, and the Canadian National Gallery bought the original of the illustration entitled 'The Three Decker.'

Shortly before he started to work on *A Song of the English* Heath Robinson had put his business affairs in the hands of A. E. Johnson, who had started an artists agency in 1906. He was beginning to find the business side of his work more and more onerous, and wanted to be free to concentrate on drawing and painting. The drawings for *A Song of the English* were the first to bear the label of the Agency on the back and to be given serial numbers which, by the time of Heath Robinson's death ran into thousands. The two men became close friends and Johnson was responsible for developing the broad range of outlets for Heath Robinson's work that was to ensure his continued success in a changing market over the years. Other artists who used the same agency at various times included H. M. Bateman, Lionel Edwards, Steven Spurrier and Bruce Bairnsfather. Interviewed for *The Strand Magazine* in April 1944, Mr. Ernest Boot of A. E. Johnson Ltd. said that of the Agency's artists 'Heath Robinson always comes out on top as far as revenue is concerned'.

On 6th May 1910, King Edward VII died, and to mark the occasion Kipling wrote fifty lines of verse under the title *The Dead King*. With the help of a number of decorative borders and vignettes drawn by Heath

Robinson, Hodder & Stoughton managed to turn this verse into a forty-eight page book. This volume, which has no less than twenty-five blank pages, is a splendid example of opportunist publishing.

In a letter to Heath Robinson in May 1910 Kipling wrote:

> *On no account must decoration become illustration absolute simplicity imperative.* I rely on you to see that this is so: no matter how you may be pressed to illustrate with pictures. The verses are not fitted for illustration in any sense and I want the borders etc. as rigidly simple and morbid as you can make them.

Heath Robinson certainly complied with this request.

Even as he executed these drawings to commemorate the death of England's monarch, another king was coming to life in Heath Robinson's thoughts, the King of Troy, who was to have such an influence on his career over the next decade.

2

Fantasy Illustration

Heath Robinson had married Josephine Latey in 1903 and their first child, Joan, was born in June the following year. In April 1908 their first son, Oliver, was born and shortly afterwards they moved from their flat in Holloway to a house at Hatch End near the village of Pinner in what was then rural Middlesex. It was here that their next two children were born, Alan in October 1909 and Quentin in March 1912. Children therefore played a great part in their lives at this time and often of a morning the Robinson's peace would be invaded by the children asking their father to tell them stories. These might have been tales of Ortho the ornithologist or have told more of 'The Wiles of Willy Willy', both of which had been the subjects of cartoon series in *The Sketch* in 1908. In later years his family remember hearing of the man with a wart on the back of his neck who never needed a collar stud and of the man whose knees were back to front so that he never knew whether he was coming or going.

Shortly after moving to Pinner Heath Robinson gave up his London studio in Carey Street to work at home. The children were always welcome in his new studio and it was natural that the next book that he illustrated was a children's story which featured many of the strange characters that he had invented. Its title was originally 'The King of Troy', and in 1910 he prepared a dummy with examples of both text and illustrations to show to publishers. Whether it was offered to Hodder & Stoughton is not known, but if so they must have refused it, for on 22nd November Heath Robinson signed a contract with Constable & Co. for a book of about sixteen stories which were to be more or less connected and to be illustrated with about sixteen coloured plates and one hundred and twenty drawings. These were to be delivered to the publishers by 31st December, 1911, and for them Heath Robinson was to receive the sum of £300. He was also entitled to six presentation copies of the book. The final clause in the contract committed Heath Robinson to offer the publishers his next two books 'upon such terms as shall be justified by the sale of the present book'.

By the time it was completed, the title of the book had been changed to *Bill the Minder*. The story, like *Uncle Lubin*, is a loosely linked episodic narrative whose hero, Bill, is also a child-minder, but there the resemblance ends, for unlike Lubin, Bill is a champion minder. At the great annual Minding Tournament held by the Duke to celebrate his birthday Bill has carried off all of the prizes, much to the rage of his rivals. These included a gold mounted feeding bottle, presented by the Duke, for minding seventeen tooth-cutters and three indigesters and sending them all to sleep in three hours and forty-five minutes. When Bill finally carried off the great cup for remaining shut up in a bathing machine with twelve vaccinated children for twelve hours the other minders so disgraced themselves in their rage that they were no longer trusted by the mothers of the district and Bill gained a monopoly of minding.

Having thus set the scene, the book goes on to describe the adventures of Bill and his charges as they first discover the deposed King of Troy asleep in a haystack, and then journey with him back to his kingdom to help him regain his throne. On their travels they meet such fantastic characters as the Ancient Mariner, the Sicilian Char-woman, the Musician, the Lost Grocer and many others, each of whom tells the sad story of his or her life before joining the party. These characters are beautifully realised both in text and illustrations, and in this respect the book is a worthy successor to *Uncle Lubin*. The story and illustrations took eighteen months to complete and in that time must have gone through many changes. One clue to these is given in the 1911 issue of a charity publication called *The Odd Volume* published in aid of the National Book Trade Provident Society. This contains two pictures by Heath Robinson. One is a simple, and somewhat unusual pencil drawing entitled 'A Bookman', the other a coloured plate entitled 'A Christmas Carol'. The latter shows a strange little man with a pointed nose and tattered clothes sitting in the snow playing a concertina. Around him are seven or eight children wrapped in rugs and all of them are singing by the light of an old fashioned lantern. This is obviously an alternative coloured plate to the story of the musician in *Bill the Minder*, although it does not actually illustrate an event in the finally published version of the story.

The book was completed by the beginning of 1912 and in June five thousand copies of the sheets for the trade edition were printed. There was then possibly some delay with the printing of the coloured plates, since nothing more was done until September, when 500 copies of a cancel title page for the New York edition to be published by Henry Holt were run off. In October the sheets for the large paper edition were printed, together with a prospectus, and the book was in the shops at the beginning of November, in good time for the Christmas market.

It seems that Constable were experiencing cash flow problems at this time and ordered a smaller number of the expensive coloured plates to be printed than they had sheets for the book. They also had bound only a

BILL THE MINDER

Illustration from *Bill the Minder*
(Constable & Co. Ltd., 1912)

relatively small number of copies for the first issue. When these had sold they then had further copies bound up in a cheaper red cloth binding with only a tiny pictorial onlay in gold on ivory paper mounted on the front board. In order to conserve their limited stock of coloured plates this second issue had only half as many as the first, one set of 16 plates serving for two copies of the book, and the coloured plates were omitted from the list of illustrations. Even greater economy was exercised with the third issue which was bound in blue cloth printed in black and contained only four coloured plates to each volume.

In 1915 a new batch of coloured plates were printed, together with a number of cancel title pages with the words 'cheaper re-issue, 1915', on the verso. These were used for what is generally regarded as the second edition which was issued in blue cloth with a tiny fragment of the coloured frontispiece mounted on the front board and with the full set of sixteen coloured plates. Subsequent 'economy' issues with the new title page also appeared, with first 12 and then 9 coloured plates and these were bound in blue cloth with the gold and ivory onlay on the upper front board.

The illustrations to the book mark the beginning of a new phase in Heath Robinson's work, in which fantasy is the predominent element. This is nowhere more clearly illustrated than in the frontispiece, which was also mounted on the cover of the first issue. In a large plate, which almost fills its mount, over fifty children tumble or float through the air surrounded by falling roses. They are painted in rich hues of red, orange and blue against a pale golden sky and the whole is a masterpiece of composition. In another coloured plate entitled 'The King of Troy compelled to ask his way' the King has on his back an enormous bundle tied with various ropes and with a worn umbrella, a kettle and a cooking pot hanging on the outside. The King's gold crown is secured under his chin with a green scarf, whilst round his neck hang a pair of scissors and an egg-timer. In this picture the three children of whom he is asking directions are Heath Robinson's three eldest children, Joan, Oliver and Alan. The group are seen standing in a field of flowers in a picture which, like many of the others in the book, is painted with a jewel-like clarity.

The line illustrations also are very finely executed and Heath Robinson had obviously lavished much time and care on their production. Of the one hundred and twenty-five drawings it is the pictorial titles to the sixteen chapters that are the best. These include 'The Ancient Mariner' with his 'interesting, absent-minded and inseparable companion', the delightful drawing of Bill himself, one eye closed and weighed down by his charges, and Heath Robinson's own favourite, 'The Triplets'.

In 1911 when these drawings were being made Heath Robinson was interviewed for *The Sketch* magazine to which he regularly contributed his humorous drawings. One of the photographs accompanying the interview showed him using Oliver, then three years old, as his model, and his own children and those of his brothers must have provided many subjects for the illustrations to *Bill the Minder*. In the interview he said that although

> ...I do not use models when I am actually making a drawing...I find them very good when studying. This boy of mine often sits for me.

He also said that if he wanted a particularly eccentric pose he would act as his own model with the aid of a mirror.

With regard to the text of the book, Heath Robinson was very modest. Writing in 1917 to O. M. Badcock, with whom he had studied at the Royal Academy Schools, he said that in writing the book he had attempted something beyond his powers. He felt that

> ...it was not a book for children and that they would not understand it, or else be bored terribly. *Uncle Lubin* in my mind is from this point of view far superior. But then I am only in the same boat as most writers of books for children, who have an eye all the time on the kind Uncle or Aunt who is going to make the purchase and who so often do not understand children.

Perhaps he was right and this is one reason why the book is so much sought after by adult collectors today.

Also published for Christmas 1912 was a Ward Lock children's annual called *Happy Hearts*. This included a cover design and two plates by Heath Robinson all lithographed in full colour. The cover design shows a large toboggan conveying an elderly lady in a bonnet and eight young children down a snow-covered slope at some speed. A small boy has just fallen from the back of the toboggan, whilst a girl in Victorian dress with a large muff is pulling a small sledge up the hill in the foreground. The two coloured plates are reminiscent of Lubin's trip to the moon. In one a group of children sit on top of a much patched balloon dangling a wooden bird on a string which a man in the basket below is attempting to shoot, whilst in the other four children sitting on the lower part of a crescent moon fishing have inadvertently caught an old lady on the end of their line and she is suspended above a snow-covered landscape. One of the photographs in *The Sketch* shows Heath Robinson at his easel, smartly dressed in suit, collar and tie, at work on this illustration. All three pictures are well printed in strong, bright colours, and in each effective use is made of a dark blue sky, studded either with stars or snowflakes, as background. The book also includes coloured plates by

John Hassall, G. E. Studdy and Louis Wain, but it is the cover design by Heath Robinson that is the most pleasing.

Following the publication of *Bill the Minder*, Constable asked Heath Robinson to illustrate a new edition of *Hans Andersen's Fairy Tales*, to be published in a similar format. It was the third time that Heath Robinson had illustrated *Hans Andersen's Fairy Tales* and he said that this time he attempted to bring out the happier aspects of the stories.

The coloured plates for the book are among the best that Heath Robinson ever made. In them he achieved that combination of the familiar and the fantastic that appeals so much to children. This is particularly true of the illustrations in which the tiny, magical figure of Tommelise is seen riding on the back of a swallow or talking to mice that are drawn with great realism. The magical qualities of flying are evoked in the pure fantasy of the colour plates to 'Elfin Mount' and 'The Little Mermaid' with their delicate ethereal colouring, or in a more believable, but no less dreamlike picture of three children on a swing for 'the Snow Queen'. However the most strangely haunting of the coloured pictures is that to 'The Wild Swans' illustrating the passage in which Elise whispered to the roses in the thick hedge outside her house "Who is more beautiful than you?" The roses shake their heads and say "Elise". The girl's face has a serene and mystical expression, which contrasts with the severe profile of the peasant's wife sitting in the background reading her hymn book. The whole composition has a mediaeval quality. It is a disturbing picture and the unhappy face of the boy in the bottom corner indicates that he too senses something strange and fey in the air.

The book is one rare occasion on which Heath Robinson's coloured plates are more successful than his line drawings. The latter show signs of haste, especially when one sees the originals, and are in general much less finely drawn than those for 'Bill the Minder'. Even so he had time to try something new, and the silhouettes illustrating 'The Marsh King's Daughter' and 'The Emperor's New Clothes' are particularly effective.

The first proofs of the book were produced in April 1913 and in October five thousand copies of the sheets for the trade edition were printed. About half of these were bound for the first issue which appeared in a bright red cloth binding heavily blocked in gold designs depicting the storks and incorporating a white and gold panel on the front. Constable were still short of capital, and only had 100 copies of the large paper edition printed, with the result that although at Christmas 1913 copies of the limited edition of *Bill the Minder* were still available, that of *Hans Andersen's Fairy Tales* had already sold out. There was a cheaper re-issue of the book in 1917 bound in red cloth printed with the original designs in dark red. This is made up from the balance of the first printing with cancel title pages.

In March 1923, presumably still short of funds, Constable offered the rights to both *Bill the Minder* and *Hans Andersen* to Hodder & Stoughton for the sum of £200 the pair. The deal was concluded in April and by the autumn Hodder & Stoughton had published a new edition of the *Hans Andersen* in their 'Golden Gift Book' series. An edition of *Bill the Minder* in the same series followed in 1924. Both books were reset in a slightly smaller format and the quality of printing was not as good as the original editions. The *Hans Andersen* was reprinted on large paper for the Boots Pure Drug Company in 1927, and a very large number of copies of this edition were sold. At the time of writing new editions of both books have recently been republished by Hodder & Stoughton.

The years from 1910 until the start of the First World War must have been very happy ones for Heath Robinson. He took great pleasure in his garden, and in the society of his neighbours, among whom was the artist Bert Thomas with whom he found much in common and who became a lifelong friend. Among the interests they shared were the countryside, old houses and young children, all of which they had at Hatch End and Pinner. His brother Tom also lived close by and many a pleasant evening must have been spent by the two brothers and their friends in the Queen's Head in Pinner village. This inn with its old oak panels and timbered ceilings was a favourite with them and sported a sign-board painted by Tom. They were often joined by friends from London for walks in the surrounding countryside and eventually formed a walking club known as The Frothfinders Federation of which their brother Charles was also an active member. Heath Robinson's chief memories of their walks are of good ale, beef, vegetables, friendship and song. One of their companions on the walks was S. Jacobs, a friend from Heath Robinson's London days with whom he had collaborated in illustrating Ascot R. Hope's book of children's stories *Tales for Toby* some years earlier. At this time Jacobs could little have thought that he would shortly be stationed in Suffolk as a member of 2/25 Cyclist Battalion, The London Regiment, sleeping under canvas and rising at 5 am. each morning.

The war was to have a less drastic effect on the life of Heath Robinson who made his contribution to the national effort through his pen. The highly beneficial effect that his cartoons had on the morale of members of all of the armed services is testified by the enormous number of letters he received offering suggestions for drawings, asking for contributions to battalion magazines or just thanking him for bringing a little humour into the wretched existence of the average soldier in the trenches. He responded

'*Titania.* To dance our ringlets to the whistling wind.'
A Midsummer Night's Dream (Constable & Co. Ltd., 1914)

'*Oberon*. Trip we after the night's shade.'
A Midsummer Night's Dream (Constable & Co. Ltd., 1914)

to these letters in a typically generous way, sending copies of his books and even original drawings to those who asked, and in 1915 he designed a Christmas card for the 3rd Division. This showed a German soldier with a Father Christmas coat draped over his uniform dropping bombs into the stockings of sleeping British soldiers. The card was extremely popular and the 30,000 copies that were printed proved too few to meet the demand for them.

Heath Robinson's humorous work had been gaining in popularity since the first examples in *The Bystander* and *The Sketch*, although some of these early products seem to have very little humour in them today, and bear little resemblance to his better known work from 1914 on. Much of the humour seems to depend either on the misdirection of Cupid's arrows, or on the presence of skinny featherless birds. Some of them also exhibit a strangely macabre streak, such as the set of six drawings published in *Pearson's Magazine* in December 1909 entitled, 'A Few Virtues'. The last of these, illustrating self-sacrifice, shows a sailor with a plump lady on board a raft. There being no other source of sustenance available, this worthy salt has just amputated his own leg and is putting it into a cooking pot heated by a candle! It is strange to think that the hand that produced these quaint and often eccentric drawings was about to illustrate one of Shakespeare's greatest plays, and in doing so produce one of the outstanding illustrated books of the twentieth century.

It was shortly after *Hans Andersen* had first been published that Heath Robinson submitted to Constable some sample drawings, made up into a dummy book, for an illustrated edition of Shakespeare's comedy of *A Midsummer Night's Dream*. This met with the publisher's approval and on 16th April a contract was signed. Looking back Heath Robinson said:

> The old Greek stories of the Wedding of Theseus and Hippolyta; of Pyramus and Thisbe and of life in Ancient Athens as seen through English eyes bewitched me. All of these and their strangely harmonious combination with everything that was lovely, and humorous too, in our English countryside filled me with enchantment. I was ambitious enough to try to express something of this in my drawings and make them a record of this, the most wonderful moonlight night in fantasy.

He was now forty-one years old and at the height of his powers as an illustrator, and this book was to be his finest achievement. In it he consolidated all that he had learnt during the past eighteen years, and in particular was able fully to realize the lessons that he had learnt in illustrating *The Poems of Edgar Allen Poe*.

As with *Twelfth Night*, Heath Robinson set out to recreate the atmosphere of the play rather than to provide a pictorial record of the

'*Bottom*. I will move storms, I will condole in some measure.'
A Midsummer Night's Dream (Constable & Co. Ltd., 1914)

action, this time with a subject that gave him greater scope for his imagination. It is the black and white illustrations that dominate the book and they fall into two main groups, the woodland scenes and the drawings of the rustics. In the woodland scenes Heath Robinson has developed a decorative style of drawing foliage which was first used by Beardsley in a number of his drawings for *The Savoy*, and of which his cover design for the first issue is typical. Heath Robinson started to refine the technique in the drawings to Poe's poems, for example in the illustration to 'Lenore', whilst his brother Charles had used a similar treatment in one or two of the drawings to *A Sensitive Plant* in 1911. In *A Midsummer Night's Dream* the style is refined further and combined with solid black skies and strong foreground patterns of wild flowers or horse chestnut leaves to produce a series of drawings that have great depth and variety of texture. These provide the ideal setting for that 'most wonderful moonlight night in fantasy'.

In sharp contrast are the series of pictures of the rustic characters Quince, Snug, Bottom, Flute, Snout and Starveling. They are drawn with great economy of line, with little or no supporting detail in the background or foreground. These compositions depend on the placing of the figures on an otherwise blank page in a style that derives from Japanese woodcuts. One first meets the characters seated on a long bench that stretches the full width of the page discussing the play they are to act out. In the foreground is a single beer mug to persuade the reader that there is a solid floor, whilst the walls of the room in Quince's house are indicated by two shadows. The grouping of the characters is perfect and each of them is a recognisable individual. This drawing and its companions perfectly express the gentle rustic humour of Shakespeare's text.

Two other drawings must be mentioned that do not fall into either of the above groups. These are the beautiful illustrations of Titania on the sea shore that illustrate the lines 'To dance our ringlets to the whistling wind' and 'Full often hath she gossip'd by my side'. Heath Robinson writing of his first sight of the sea said that he was 'thrilled by the sight of that distant horizon, and the sun shining on a sail far away'. This love of the sea shore remained with him throughout his life and was the setting for some of his best illustrations, such as the drawing to Poe's poem 'Evening Star', and especially these two in *A Midsummer Night's Dream*.

The coloured illustrations are very much an integral part of the book, providing variety of texture and tone, and if anything fulfil a supporting function in the overall scheme. With their subdued colouring and incidental subjects they add to the atmosphere of the book without becoming the focus of attention. The experiments with light that were a feature of the *Twelfth Night* illustrations continue here, as in the delicate

'He saw before him a huge building.'
The Water Babies (Constable & Co. Ltd., 1915)

frontispiece showing Titania borne by her fairies across the surface of the lake.

The book was published in mid October 1914 and was described by a reviewer in *The Times Literary Supplement* as:

> The most complete and beautiful specimen before us of an illustrated book as a single work of art...

The first issue appeared in a restrained but luxurious binding of grey cloth blocked with a pictorial design in gold, ochre, mauve, pink and two shades of blue. There was also a limited edition of two hundred and fifty copies on handmade paper, of which Constable had a hundred bound in vellum, blocked in gilt, for the first issue. The trade edition cost 12s 6d and the limited edition 31s 6d. At the time the book was published it was commonly believed that the First World War would end by Christmas, but as it dragged on over the next four years sales of the book must have been depressed. A second issue was produced during the war in a cheaper blue cloth binding printed in black, and in 1919 the remainder of both the trade and limited editions were bound up in cloth backed green boards, the trade edition selling in this form at 7s 6d. In 1923 Constable offered the book to Hodder & Stoughton, along with *Hans Andersen* and *Bill the Minder*, but they declined, presumably because it did not fit into their 'Golden Gift Book' series which was aimed at a juvenile market. The book was therefore not reprinted until 1976 when Minerva brought out a facsimile edition. This was without colour plates and was printed with much reduced margins, but was nevertheless an attractive and well produced book.

On the same day that Heath Robinson contracted to illustrate *A Midsummer Night's Dream* he also signed a contract to illustrate Charles Kingsley's story of *The Water Babies* for Constable. The first two coloured plates and twelve line drawings were to be delivered by the end of February 1914 and the balance of the work by the end of June. This was an ideal text for him, providing the opportunity to combine two of his favourite subjects, children and the sea. It was also an obvious choice, following on from the illustrations to 'The Little Mermaid' in *Hans Andersen* for which he had provided two coloured plates and seven line drawings.

In style, the illustrations for *The Water Babies* are very close to those for *Hans Andersen*. The similarity starts with the frontispieces for the two books, one showing a baby sitting in a water-lily looking at a stork, and the other with a water baby kneeling in the water watching a dragon fly. The similarities continue, with the 'little white lady in her bed' identifiable as 'the real princess' in Andersen, and once again there is the juxtaposition of realism and fantasy in the drawings, for example in the picture of Tom pursued by a rather vicious looking otter. Only occasionally does a hint of the *Midsummer Night's Dream* drawings appear, and then it is usually in the very attractive coloured plates, rather than in the line drawings.

At the time the book was commissioned it was probably intended that it should be published in a lavish gift-book format like *Bill the Minder* and *Hans Andersen*, but with the outbreak of war plans would have changed and the book eventually appeared on the market in the autumn of 1915 as a rather modest octavo volume. The war had spelt the end of the de luxe gift book and although a few publishers were to attempt to revive the format, these later editions were but a poor echo of the originals. Heath Robinson wrote that even in the autumn of 1914:

> Publishers were beginning to restrict their enterprise within narrower channels, and these were all connected with the war. There was now no demand for purely artistic productions, for new editions of Shakespeare or other classics, unless they bore some connections with the all absorbing topic.

There was therefore no direct successor to *A Midsummer Night's Dream*, and by the time a new market for well illustrated adult books was established by the private presses Heath Robinson was too strongly identified in the public mind with his humorous drawings for a 'serious' publisher to take the chance of commissioning this kind of work from him.

However, even in wartime, and perhaps especially then, the market for children's books continued, and it was here that Heath Robinson's career as an illustrator continued for the next few years, alongside a great deal of work in the popular magazines. These published both fairy tale illustrations and cartoons, and it was during the first world war that his reputation as a humorous artist was consolidated and his first books of humorous drawings published.

Anyone who, in December 1914, was looking for interesting and varied reading material and had a shilling to spend could hardly do better than to invest in the 'Grand Double Christmas Number' of *The Strand Magazine*. This consisted of two hundred pages of text and pictures as well as eighty pages of advertisements. Inside he would find the latest episode of 'The Valley of Fear' by A. Conan Doyle and 'Parted Ways' by P. G. Wodehouse, the latter illustrated by Alfred Leete. There were other stories by such authors as Edgar Wallace and W. W. Jacobs and an article explaining how a process block was made, illustrated with photographs of *The Strand's* own equipment. For children there was a story by

Norah M. Craggs called 'The Death of Rancing Roarer' which was illustrated with four fine line drawings by W. Heath Robinson.

The Strand Magazine, founded in 1891 by George Newnes, had had a tradition of including in each issue one good children's story or an episode of a children's serial. In the early years these were usually translations of foreign stories and most were illustrated by H. R. Millar. During the first decade of the new century the children's pages came to be dominated by E. Nesbit, with stories such as 'The Phoenix and the Carpet', 'The Psammead', 'Wet Magic' and dozens more, again mainly illustrated by Millar. However, in 1914 Nesbit's husband died and she was taken very ill, so *The*

'When did the king look funnier than when he was asleep?' and Rancing Roarer burst into a guffaw of laughter.'
Illustration from
'The Death of Rancing Roarer',
The Strand
Magazine,
1914

Strand Magazine had
to look elsewhere for its
children's stories, publishing
some translations of old tales
from overseas and some newly
written stories by other writers.

The first art editor of *The
Strand Magazine* was W. H. J.
Boot who held the post for
twenty years from 1891 to 1910.
He had become acquainted with
Heath Robinson in 1908, when
he published a series of comic
drawings under the title 'Why I
am Not a Criminal' that featured
such characters as 'the kind-
eyed winkle-Pilferer of
Paddington Green'. He was
followed by his son J. Sydney
Boot of whom Heath Robinson said:

'Seven
times the
head flew round
the chamber.'
Illustration from
'The Ogres of Ojejama',
The Strand Magazine, 1915.

... I was always pleased to feel that he had a kindly interest in me and
my work. It seemed that he extended his kindness to all he dealt with
and little enough to himself. I, and many another artist too, lost a friend
when he died.

Sydney Boot was perceptive enough to see in Heath Robinson the ideal
illustrator for *The Strand Magazine's* children's stories and during 1915

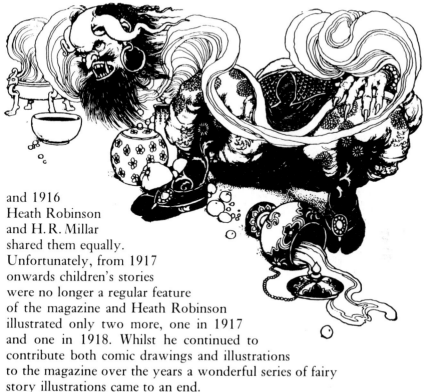

and 1916
Heath Robinson
and H. R. Millar
shared them equally.
Unfortunately, from 1917
onwards children's stories
were no longer a regular feature
of the magazine and Heath Robinson
illustrated only two more, one in 1917
and one in 1918. Whilst he continued to
contribute both comic drawings and illustrations
to the magazine over the years a wonderful series of fairy
story illustrations came to an end.

Between 1914 and 1918 Heath Robinson provided illustrations to a total of fourteen children's stories in *The Strand Magazine*. They were executed with great care and attention to detail. In subject they present an ideal combination of fantasy and humour, whilst in execution they are a blend of all the best elements in the last four books that he had illustrated. The compositions show great originality, freeing themselves entirely from the constraints of the page format and spreading at will across one or two pages, leaving the text to find space around them. The high standard set in the first of the stories was maintained throughout and taken as a whole they represent one of his finest achievements in the field of fairy tale illustration, possibly even surpassing the drawings for *Bill the Minder*. It seems that the combination of a good, unfamiliar story with a limited requirement to make two, three or four drawings at a time inspired his best work.

The drawings to 'The Death of Rancing Roarer' are typical. The first of them, which occupies three-quarters of the first double page opening of the story, shows a king who was 'simply enormous — terribly fat, without

a corner anywhere.' He is surrounded by a number of his subjects, in this case seven children and three old men, who 'could not help laughing whenever they saw him.' This king's lands were being plundered by an ogre, who is admirably portrayed in the second drawing. He is obviously related to the giant who blew Vammer-dopper over mountains and seas in *Uncle Lubin* and is one of an original family of giants and ogres created by Heath Robin-son. An offer by the king of half of his kingdom to who-ever rids him of this ogre failed to attract any help, and so the king set out to deal with him himself. When he announced this intention his worst fears were realised, since 'the roars of laughter were heard miles out of town, and

'"Would you jest with me, you pitiful little object?"
said the goblin . . .

one of his ministers dislocated his jaw.' However the
king triumphed in the end and his subjects were then
duly respectful. In the other two illustrations to this
story Heath Robinson made skilful use of sharply
drawn foregrounds with silhouette backgrounds.
The last drawing in particular with its procession
of tiny silhouette figures winding across the
double page openings is a masterly invention
which must have fascinated young readers of
the story.
Many of the stories that H.R. Millar illustrated
for the *Strand* were reprinted in books such as
The Silver Fairy Book or *Queen Mab's Fairy Realm*,
but no such happy fate awaited Heath Robinson's
work. Instead, most of his pictures were used to
illustrate stories in *Playbox Annual* for the years
1917 to 1922, many of them illustrating stories
other than the ones for which they were intended.
They were badly reprinted, some of them in pale
colours, and in many cases the carefully designed
relationship between drawing, text and overall
page size has been completely lost. Sadly,
when Hamlyn reprinted the drawings in
The Heath

"No," was the answer; "I have come to fight with you for the princess."'
Illustration from 'The Sea Goblins', *Strand Magazine*, 1915

Robinson Illustrated Story Book in 1979 they used the *Playbox Annuals* as their source and the book by no means does justice to the originals. It also omits some of the best of the drawings for *The Strand Magazine*, such as the illustrations to the Japanese story 'The Ogres of Ojejama' or the illustration of the 'Sea Goblins' from the story of the same name. In the latter case the other two pictures that Heath Robinson made for the story are used to illustrate the much inferior tale of 'The Greedy Boy and the Princess'. No doubt sea goblins and ogres were thought to be too frightening for the young readers of *Playbox Annual*.

In December 1915 *Pearson's Magazine* published a children's story called 'Biddulph. The Tale of a Magic Pool' which was both written and illustrated by Heath Robinson. It tells of Nod and Glynneth and their perpetually wretched son Biddulph, who live on a bleak rock ever so far up near the north pole. The headpiece to the story perfectly depicts this young boy standing on a beach, hands thrust into his pockets and a deep frown on his face. His only friends are the fairies that haunt the rock. Another drawing, reminiscent of *A Midsummer Night's Dream*, shows these fairies who 'used to try all they knew to entice him from his grief', flying in procession across a double page spread whilst the wretched boy stands unmoved at the foot of the picture with his back to the reader. Finally the boy is induced to smile when he sees his own face reflected in a woodland pool, and when his parents transfer this
pool to the garden of their house,
bucketful by bucketful,

'There came out
two giants armed
with huge cudgels,
who laid about
them vigorously.'
Illustration from
'The Rusty Pot and
the Wooden Balls',
The Strand Magazine, 1916

their troubles are gone forever. The drawings for
this story seem to have less fantasy and more of a homely quality than
those for *The Strand Magazine*, probably because Heath Robinson was
illustrating his own text. The name Biddulph was used for one of the
characters in *Bill the Minder* and the story doubtless derives from those
that he told to his own children, the figure of Biddulph being based on his
elder sons Oliver and Alan who would have been seven and six years old
respectively at the time.

The year before the start of the First World War Heath Robinson had
the chance to broaden still further the scope of his illustration when he
was commissioned by the composer and music teacher Walter Carroll to
design the cover for a book of music called *The Countryside*. He produced
an attractive design, drawn in the style of the *Midsummer Night's Dream*
illustrations, which so pleased the composer that he had the original
framed and kept it on the wall of his music room throughout his life.

Headpiece for 'Biddulph.
A Tale of a Magic Pool'.
Pearson's Magazine, 1915

Unfortunately the publishers did not do justice to the
design by printing the cover in pale green on white.
In 1916 Carroll asked Heath Robinson to design a cover
and title page for another set of pieces entitled *Forest
Fantasies* which he described as being '... woven from the mysteries of
fairyland'. The subject was ideal and the artist produced a pair of designs
that might have come straight from *A Midsummer Night's Dream*. This
time the publishers did them full justice, in spite of the problems of
wartime production, printing in deep black on white.

In February 1916 Heath Robinson started work on a set of illustrations
for Walter de la Mare's book of children's poems *Peacock Pie* for Constable
& Co. The original contract is lost, but in a letter to the publishers his
agent, A. E. Johnson, asks for a copy of the book so that work can start on
the illustrations, which were expected to be finished by the end of May.
This was the first book for which illustrations had been commissioned
since the start of the war, and was consequently designed to be published
in a more modest format than the previous books that Heath Robinson
had illustrated for Constable. Only one coloured plate was called for, to
be used as the frontispiece, together with one line drawing for each of the
eighty-two poems, title page, half titles, endpaper and binding designs.

Sending a copy of the book to a friend Heath Robinson wrote:

> Some of [the poems] are very reminiscent of Robert Louis Stevenson,
> but there is nevertheless a wonderful originality in them. I will not bore
> you with an apology for my illustrations ... but I must say that the
> medium I was compelled to use restrains one considerably.

This implies that he was unable to fulfil some of the ideas he had for the

'Some One'
Peacock Pie (Constable & Co. Ltd., 1916)

book, but such constraints often prove an advantage for an illustrator.

Heath Robinson was generally at his best with black and white illustrations and these poems inspired a series of decorative drawings that echo the simplicity and rhythm of de la Mare's verse. The style of drawing is developed from *A Midsummer Night's Dream* with a strong emphasis

on texture and pattern. Once again his favourite themes of children and
the sea shore combine in illustrations such as that to the poem 'Sam', and
the miserable figure of Biddulph returns in the guise of 'The Bookworm'
looking no more cheerful than before. Effective use is made of circular
frames for a number of the drawings. The book is in the tradition of

'King David'
Peacock Pie (Constable & Co. Ltd., 1916)

illustrated children's poetry books started twenty years earlier by his
brother Charles with his designs for *A Child's Garden of Verses* and *Lullaby
Land*, and must have had an influence on those artists who followed,
such as E. H. Shepard illustrating A. A. Milne.

At the time Heath Robinson was illustrating *Peacock Pie* he was also, through his agent, discussing ideas for another book with Constable. His first suggestion was a new edition of Aesop's fables and there is no doubt that he would have proved an ideal illustrator for this. In his illustrations to various stories over the years, ranging from *The Giant Crab* to the drawings of birds and a lion in *The Strand Magazine* he had shown his ability to draw animal subjects. However, Contable & Co. were not confident of the commercial prospects for such a book and so Heath Robinson made two other suggestions. A.E.Johnson wrote in February 1916:

> ...Mr. Robinson suggests Perrault's Tales, which have not been overdone, so far as he is aware, as a gift book. He would propose to draw the illustrations, as regards costume, etc., more or less in the style of Perrault's period, which he thinks would provide him with very good opportunities for some charming drawings.
>
> Failing Perrault, he would like to illustrate a series of folk tales to which he has access. These are in the vein of the famous Grimm collection, being derived from Austria and Bohemia in much the same way as the Grimm stories were derived from Germany. The collection was published some 25 to 30 years ago and is little known.

This latter collection was Vernaleken's *In the Land of Marvels* that had been translated by Edwin Johnson and published by Sonnenschein & Co. in 1884. Heath Robinson was introduced to the book when he was asked to illustrate 'The Hat Full of Soldiers', a story from Vernaleken's collection that appeared in *The Strand Magazine* in January 1916, just a month before A.E.Johnson's letter to Constable. However, it was the suggestion of *Perrault's Tales* that appealed to Constable, and sadly it was not until 1934 that Heath Robinson had the opportunity to illustrate the Bohemian tales.

Heath Robinson had been asked to work within a price of one hundred pounds by Constable. For that sum he offered six coloured illustrations and from forty to fifty line drawings, of which a considerable proportion would be full page. He said he could probably complete the book by the end of June, which would have been in time for the Christmas market in 1916. However, first Constable had to find a suitable text. They considered using the edition that had been published by the Clarendon Press in 1888 and was edited by Andrew Lang, but for some reason this was rejected and it was decided to commission a new translation to be written by Heath Robinson's agent, A.E.Johnson. Then there was the question of how many tales to use, and whether to include the morals. It was decided that to Perrault's original eight stories should be added one by Mme de Beaumont and two by Mme. d'Aulnoy but that the morals should be omitted.

The lessons learnt in illustrating *A Midsummer Night's Dream* continued to be developed in the best of the drawings for this new book, but whereas the previous two books had drawn on the woodland scenes, here Heath Robinson explores the possibilities of the economical outlines and minimal backgrounds that he used for the scenes featuring the rustic characters in that book. Typical is the illustration 'They all fell asleep' to the story of 'The Sleeping Beauty in the Wood', the first in the book. 'Tom Thumb' he illustrated in the same style, and this story inspired a typical Heath Robinson ogre who appears to be a close relative of Rancing Roarer. The picture of Tom journeying home in his seven league boots laden with all the ogre's wealth is one of the most delightful in the book. A few pages on from this story one comes to the startling picture of 'Ricky of the Tuft.' This is the first of five drawings in which the use of blank space is taken to the limit with brilliant effect. In each case the illustration consists of one or two figures drawn in decorative line and set in a frame with no background or foreground. These pictures rely on the tension between figures or between a figure and the frame for their success. In one of the illustrations, the figure of Cinderella seems to be running through the frame, breaking it on either side, whilst in the picture of Cinderella's stepmother and father Heath Robinson has used the composition from the coloured plate to 'The Respectable Gentleman' in *Bill the Minder* but executed in a much simpler style. The last drawing in this new style is the most effective of all, and shows Bluebeard brandishing a sabre above his wife's head. The drama of the scene is heightened by the lack of background, and both figures seem to stand on a solid floor although we are given no other clue to its presence than that it supports their weight. The reviewer in *The Studio* magazine wrote of the book when it was first published:

> ... not only are these drawings remarkable for the beauty of their line, but in many of them this beauty is enhanced by the artist's appreciation of the value of blank space — an aesthetic factor to which the Japanese attach so much importance.

Less than half of the drawings were in the styles described above. One of the longest stories in the book is 'Beauty and the Beast' and in illustrating it Heath Robinson was unable to settle on a suitable style. The first drawing might have come from *The Water Babies*, the second is in his simple 'rustics' style, the third could have been made for the 1899 *Andersen's Fairy Tales* and in the fourth one sees the beast for the first time and finds he is borrowed from brother Charles's *Big Book of Fairy Tales*. The final drawing is unlike anything else that he ever drew and is best forgotten. This lack of stylistic unity in the drawings for 'Beauty

'Laden with all the ogre's wealth',
Old Time Stories (Constable & Co. Ltd., 1921)

'Brandishing the cutlass aloft.'
Old Time Stories (Constable & Co. Ltd., 1921)

and the Beast' is typical of the volume as a whole and in spite of the presence of a number of fine drawings the book must be accounted a failure. The six coloured plates do little to redeem the situation, being little more than line drawings with thin washes of colour, and poorly reproduced.

The book was finally published in 1921 and Constable made an attempt to recreate the luxury of the pre-war gift books. The binding for the small first issue was in deep red cloth with a circular white onlay blocked in gilt, rather like those used on *Hans Andersen* and *Peacock Pie*. The coloured plates were on beige card mounts and although the quality of the paper and the black and white printing were not as good as in the earlier books, the volume had a feel of quality. However, when subsequent issues appeared the white onlay had gone, the beige card mounts had been replaced by sugar paper in a dirty shade of green and evidence of cost cutting could not be disguised.

During the five years that elapsed between the first discussion of *Old Time Stories* and its publication Heath Robinson worked mainly for periodicals. Most of this work was humorous and much of it cartoons. Following the success of the collections of cartoons from *The Sketch* and other magazines that had been published under the titles *Some Frightful War Pictures* and *Hunlikely!* he prepared a book of original line drawings called *The Saintly Hun; a Book of German Virtues*. Many of these delightful drawings were produced in the same style as he used for *Peacock Pie*, whilst the remainder are in silhouette, and they illustrate such virtues as courtesy, shown by German officers leaving cards on a tank newly arrived in the district.

One of the periodicals to which he contributed at this time was *Out and Away* which was published by J. Birch and Heath Robinson's younger brother George. This was described as 'A Posy of Traveller's Joy' and its theme was travel, with a strong emphasis on motoring. It was a lavishly illustrated magazine, and as well as Heath Robinson and his brother Tom, its artists included Lionel Edwards, H. M. Bateman, H. R. Millar, C. E. Brock, Fougasse and the distinctive R. E. Higgins. Well known writers were not so numerous, but included Max Pemberton, Arthur Machen and G. K. Chesterton. Heath Robinson contributed eight illustrations to a story by William Caine, as well as three sets of motoring cartoons. However it is doubtful whether he or the other contributors received much in the way of payment for their labours since the magazine folded after three issues. The unsold stock was bound up and sold off in volume form.

3

A Change of Direction

In the spring of 1918 Heath Robinson and his family moved from Pinner to Cranleigh, a small town in the heart of the Surrey countryside. The move was made, he said, to enable the whole family to banish the frightfulness of the war in all its forms from their minds and to lead peaceful country lives. It was there, in 1919, that his youngest child, Tom, was born. The three older boys went to Cranleigh School, which was founded in 1863 and was one of the better minor public schools, while his daughter Joan attended St. Catherine's School in nearby Bramley. They were all day pupils and so the pattern of family life was not disrupted by one or other member departing for boarding school. Heath Robinson was a shy and simple man, closest to his children while they were still young and so the ten years they spent at Cranleigh after the First World War were among their happiest.

With his move to Cranleigh Heath Robinson became more cut off from the general run of the London art and publishing world and therefore reliant on his agent A.E. Johnson to find commissions for him. Fortunately postal communications were reliable and rapid and it was mainly by this means that the two kept in touch. However, he was not completely isolated from the society of his fellow artists. When he first moved to Cranleigh, Lawson Wood was living there and Bertram Prance had a house in the nearby village of Rudgewick. Both Bert Thomas, who had been a neighbour in Pinner, and Alfred Leete had children at Cranleigh School and so frequently had occasion to visit, and H.M. Bateman would come over from his house in Reigate.

Another regular means of contact with other artists was through his two clubs, The London Sketch Club and The Savage. The London Sketch Club had been formed at the beginning of the century and provided a place where members could meet each Friday, partly to enjoy good food, drink and congenial company, but more importantly to fulfil the function suggested by the name of the club, the practice of rapid memory sketching to given subjects. Walter Churcher, writing in *The Studio* magazine in 1915 said that the club kitchen produced 'steak puddings and roast sirloin having no rivals save at "The Cheese" and "Simpsons"'. To judge from the list of members at that time, which included John Hassall, Cecil Aldin, Claude Shepperson, Harry Rountree, Edmund Dulac, H.M. Bateman,

G. E. Studdy, Willy Pogany and many other fine artists, the sketching must have been of an equally high standard. Heath Robinson had been elected a member in 1910, soon after he gave up his London studio and moved to Pinner, having been proposed by Frank Reynolds and seconded by his agent A. E. Johnson.

He became a member of his second club, The Savage, in 1924, having been proposed by Bert Thomas. This was an older club that had been founded at the suggestion of George Augustus Sala in 1857. Membership was limited to professionals in the categories of Literature, Art, Drama, Science and Music. A sixth category, Law, was added in 1956. The main activity of the club was to organise a series of Saturday Suppers that took place during the winter and spring months. For each supper one of the members took the chair and often there would be a guest of honour. Each occasion was marked by a souvenir menu card, usually drawn by one of the artist members, and many of the originals of these are stored in a large Tibetan wine cooler in the club. They include a number by Heath Robinson, the earliest of which dates from 1911, some thirteen years before he became a member. Another, from 1938, marked a dinner at which the eminent scientist, Sir James Jeans, was the guest of honour.

Invitation card to a Sketch Club function

He was so delighted with the menu card, which showed an early attempt to split the atom with 'Heath Robinson' machinery, that he asked the artist to let him have the original, promising that it would find an honoured place in his room. Similar cards were also produced for Sketch Club functions and Churcher reproduces one by Heath Robinson for a 'smoking conversazione' on 4th December, 1913 which shows an artist being tempted by Pan with a pipe in one hand and a foaming tankard in the other.

One of the commissions that A. E. Johnson secured for Heath Robinson soon after his move to Cranleigh was from the newly formed publishing house of Jonathan Cape. It was for over four hundred drawings to illustrate a new edition of the complete works of Shakespeare. Work on the project had started by January 1921, when Cape took a number of the drawings to America in the hope of finding a publisher there with whom he could share the cost. By the end of 1921 the commission was not completed, although the four hundred drawings originally contracted for had been delivered and A. E. Johnson reported that Cape and his partner Wren Howard were delighted with them. In February 1922 a further consignment of drawings was delivered and at the beginning of March Heath Robinson received £200 on account for the work to date.

The precise format in which the edition was planned to be published is not clear, but there are a few pointers to aid speculation. A request from Cape for a drawing on every page was rejected because it would have required upwards of 3000 drawings. This implies either a set of eight to twelve volumes each containing several plays, or a set of about forty slim volumes with a single play or set of poems in each. The little remaining evidence seems to favour several plays per volume. In a letter to Heath Robinson, Cape mentions that he would like a full page illustration to face the opening of each play, a choice of words that implies more than one play to a volume. Another letter from Howard requests that the pictures to run down the sides of the pages should be drawn in pairs with the same dimensions so that they could be reduced on a single block. They were to be reduced to one and a half inches width, implying a page size larger than might be expected if each play was to be published in a separate volume.

The illustrations made during 1921 were wholly in line, but in March 1922 a letter from Howard mentioned proofs he had made of some coloured illustrations. In May A. E. Johnson noted that the last two coloured subjects had been sent to Cape. It therefore appears that by this time the project had become even more ambitious and costly. The illustrations were finally completed in June 1922, but either because of lack of funds, or because of the declining market for illustrated books the edition was never published, and the present whereabouts of the original drawings and watercolours, if indeed they still exist, is a mystery. Perhaps they are lying carefully wrapped in a warehouse somewhere waiting to be discovered. One can only hope!

The completion of the Shakespeare drawings was a great relief to both the artist and his agent, since at the time Heath Robinson was overloaded with requests for his work, both in the form of cartoons to be published in weekly and monthly magazines and for advertising which was taking up more and more of his time. He was also engaged on a children's book that he had been commissioned to write and illustrate for the publishers S. W. Partridge & Co.

In the summer of 1921 he had made a set of eight full page line drawings for the book, *Peter Quip in Search of a Friend*, and these had been sent to Partridge together with a synopsis of the plot. Blocks were made from the drawings by the printers Thomas Forman & Sons and two sets of proofs of the illustrations printed on Whatman boards were sent to Heath Robinson in October 1921 for colouring. The printers then made a set of five-colour blocks from the coloured proofs. Partridge also asked Heath Robinson to colour the originals, but this he declined to do, saying that it would involve a very great deal more work with no advantage.

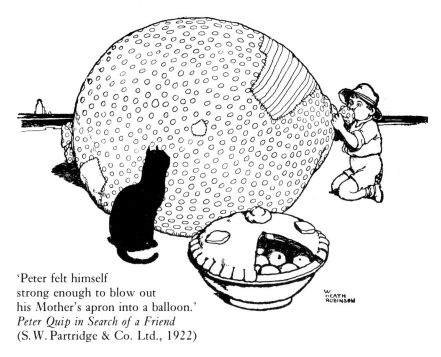

'Peter felt himself
strong enough to blow out
his Mother's apron into a balloon.'
Peter Quip in Search of a Friend
(S. W. Partridge & Co. Ltd., 1922)

'A queer little dog seized on his tattered cloak.'
Illustration from 'Treasure Trove', *Little Folks*, 1921

The book was planned to have thirty-two pages of text, which, with the eight full page illustrations, would have given one picture to every five pages. Partridge thought this insufficient, but anxious to avoid extra expense, suggested that portions of the eight drawings should be printed in line throughout the book to increase the proportion of pictures. Heath Robinson agreed to this provided that he chose which portions were to be used. In the event he did not find enough suitable material in the original drawings. He therefore made eight additional line drawings, which supplemented the eleven small portions of the original drawings that were used in the book. Partridge also said that the synopsis of the plot would soon be placed in the hands of a good writer to elaborate it, so although the book when published was wholly attributed to Heath Robinson, it was in fact ghost written.

Proofs of the coloured plates for the book were sent to Heath Robinson in March 1922 and *Peter Quip* was published in September of that year. It was an attractive volume in its bright pictorial boards and the coloured plates were beautifully printed on the same matt paper as the rest of the book. The story, like *Bill the Minder*, chronicles a journey made by a group of travellers, who in this case include a number of animals. It describes the adventures that befall the hero Peter as he searches for a friend and each adventure increases the size of his party. In both the plot and pictures for this book Heath Robinson has avoided the dangers he foresaw of producing a volume 'for the kind Uncle or Aunt who is going to make a purchase' and with the aid of a competent ghost writer has produced a story that can be both understood and loved by young children. The simple nursery format and the clear, brightly coloured illustrations make no concessions to the adult world in the way that he feared *Bill the Minder* had done. The book sold at 3s 6d and was aimed, like *Uncle Lubin*, at younger children. This fact, and the state of the book market in 1922, have combined to make it one of the hardest of Heath Robinson's books to find today.

Partridge had not proved to be an easy publisher to work for and it seems that Heath Robinson derived little pleasure from his first book for them. He therefore wrote to his agent suggesting that they should try to remove the clause in the contract committing him to a second book. Johnson's reply gives an indication of the market for illustrated books at the time. He wrote in October 1921:

> I don't think it is worth while at the moment to raise the question of the second book which you originally agreed to do. In the present state of the trade I do not think Partridge's will want to embark upon a second book for a long while yet, and consequently the provisional agreement for a second volume will probably die a natural death. There is no particular advantage in going out of one's way to kill a thing which obligingly shows signs of dying of its own accord — moreover, one never knows one's luck and there might be a day when you wished you hadn't killed it.

In the event no second book was ever published.

Early in 1922 a lady by the name of Elsie Smeaton Munro approached the publisher John Lane with a set of twelve children's stories that she had written, called *Topsy Turvy Tales*. She was acquainted with Heath Robinson and gave the publisher to understand that she could get him to illustrate her stories. Under these circumstances Lane agreed to publish them, and in June Miss Munro's brother approached A. E. Johnson to make formal arrangements for the illustrations. Lane had said that he was willing to spend one hundred guineas and wanted to know what could be done for that sum. He also said that he would like some of the drawings to be in colour. Johnson replied offering either four full page coloured pictures and twenty line drawings of various sizes, or, alternatively, one coloured drawing and from thirty to forty 'pen and inks'. Lane responded by asking for eight coloured pictures and sixteen decorative drawings. This was thought by Johnson to be too much for the money and he replied suggesting that either the price would need to be increased by twenty-five guineas or the number of coloured drawings reduced to six. Lane agreed to the latter option and in August a contract was signed for six full page drawings in colour, sixteen pen and ink drawings and odd decorations, the drawings to be delivered by the end of February 1923. However, Lane wanted the first two coloured drawings earlier, and these were delivered in November.

Unusually, Lane also insisted on posession of the original drawings. Writing on this point to Heath Robinson, who at the time was on holiday in Bognor, A. E. Johnson said:

> In the ordinary way I should drop negotiations forthwith, but, as a matter of fact, I do not see that the original drawings for this particular book will be of very much value to you. It is not as though they would be illustrations to a Classic like *Hans Andersen*, and it is unlikely that private buyers will be greatly interested in them.

The book was published the following year and was to be the last book illustrated by Heath Robinson for a decade. At least four of the pen and ink drawings for the book are now in the Metropolitan Museum of Art in New York.

The unusual qualities of the text were well summarized by a reviewer for *The Bookman* who wrote in December 1923:

> ...children will take these tales just as they are and enjoy them because they are funny and ridiculous things happen just as little people like them to happen. But older folk will realize their cleverness and perhaps writhe when they see their own caricatures. The author takes our time worn phrases and plots and conceits weaving them brilliantly into her twelve highly original stories.... To say that the illustrations are by Heath Robinson is enough bush for the good wine in this book.

When published it had, in addition to the six full page coloured illustrations, sixteen full page and twenty smaller line drawings, a typically generous interpretation of the contract. The coloured drawings are extremely attractive and in their subdued tones and skilful use of dappled lighting are reminiscent of the work of Heath Robinson's elder brother, Charles. This is particularly true of the picture that illustrates the tale of 'Peeriwinkie, the Puddock' and the beauty of this picture only adds to the irony of the story. The line drawings include a number of silhouettes and in many of the other drawings figures are depicted in the style of the cartoons that were now occupying so much of his time. Like *Old Time Stories*, this book lacks a coherent style, but a thickening of line and a simpler treatment of subject can be discerned throughout. The vivacity and tension that was apparent in the fantasy illustrations from *Bill the Minder* through to the children's stories in *The Strand Magazine* had gone and were never to return. It is hard to tell whether this was because of a change in his outlook and interests or, more likely, the changed economic climate that he had to work in after the First World War.

By 1922 the demand for fine illustrated books that had been so buoyant ten years earlier had all but disappeared. In particular, there was no longer a large market for the kind of gift book in which the illustrations were its *raison d'etre*, and the text, (usually out of copyright), an excuse for publishing a large number of beautiful pictures in black and white or colour. This resulted in some hardship for Heath Robinson's brother Charles who, in common with many illustrators at that time, had found that by 1919 his main source of income had virtually disappeared. However, Heath Robinson was more fortunate for his reputation was more widely based than that of his brother and whilst the war had brought a decline in the amount of work he found as an illustrator, it had also provided him with the opportunity to enhance his standing as a humorous artist.

He was an eminently practical man and so although he well knew that as an artist his best work would always be in the field of serious illustration, he accepted his responsibilities as a family man and turned his hand to those commissions that were available. These were either for magazines or advertizing material and in the main called upon him to exercise his talents as a humorist. It is typical of him that in every piece of work he sold one can see the same care and craftsmanship exercised, whether in an advertisement for toffees or a cartoon for a charity publication; a line drawing for a 3d weekly paper or a full page coloured plate for the Christmas number of an expensive monthly magazine.

It was Heath Robinson's increasing celebrity as a humorist that led him into the world of broadcasting. Since 1905, when one of his earliest cartoons had appeared in its pages, he had been a regular contributor to *The Bystander*, and in April 1923 an unusual competition run by that magazine introduced him to radio broadcasting. The competition was called, 'Drawings by Wireless'. Heath Robinson, speaking from the studio at London's radio station 2 L0, described to listeners a drawing he had made of the difficulties of erecting an aerial. Those wishing to participate in the competition were then invited to make a sketch in the style of Mr. Heath Robinson and to send it to *The Bystander*. The winning entry would be the one that came closest to the original drawing that had been described. A prize of ten guineas was offered and the best drawings submitted were published in a subsequent issue of the magazine. The winning entry looks more like the artist's published work than the simple sketch that he had prepared for the broadcast!

For a similar broadcast on 30th December 1925, listeners were asked to have a sheet of paper ready with numbered squares ruled on it. Heath Robinson was then able to give a sequence of instructions over the radio from which the listeners could construct a picture. Until it neared completion they had no idea what it was they were drawing, but if they had followed the instructions correctly the result was a picture of Noah's Ark with the dove perched on top of it. Cash prizes were offered to listeners for the three best sketches drawn to Heath Robinson's instructions. 15,000 entries were received and the first prize was awarded to a Mr. E. L. Taylor, "The Dog's Kennel", Woodham Lane, Addlestone, Surrey, whose drawing was published in *The Radio Times* on 22nd January, 1926. Later broadcasts included an invitation to be a guest on the popular BBC programme 'In Town Tonight', in April 1934. He was interviewed with K. M. Gleason, the inventor of an electric fly-catcher. In 1938 he made an early television appearance during which he drew and demonstrated many of his devices, finishing up with a demonstration of his new pea-splitting machine.

During the time they were living at Cranleigh the Heath Robinson family came to know the countryside well. They would take long walks through the surrounding fields and woods and on their return home the things they had seen provided the subject matter for many of the water-colours that Heath Robinson painted for his own enjoyment. Throughout his life he devoted a part of his time to imaginative watercolour painting and as opportunities to sell his serious illustrative work declined this recreational painting became more important to him. Even on holiday, usually at Waxham in Norfolk, while the rest of the family enjoyed swimming in the sea or playing on the beach, he would sit dressed in suit and collar and tie painting at his easel. In this work he was constantly experimenting with the rhythmical qualities of scenery, turning land-

'And a very good time they had too.' Illustration for *Peter Quip in Search of a Friend* (S.W. Partridge & Co. Ltd., 1922)

'No giant could behold such distress unmoved.'
Topsy Turvy Tales (John Lane the Bodley Head Ltd., 1923)

scapes into flowing patterns, and with the various qualities of light, shade and colour, extending for his own satisfaction the ideas he had first started to develop in his illustrations for books such as *Twelfth Night* and *A Midsummer Night's Dream*.

A more remunerative respite from the constant need to be funny came from time to time over the next fifteen years with commissions to provide serious illustrations to short stories and articles in *Nash's Pall Mall Magazine* and its sister publication *Good Housekeeping*. Both of these monthly magazines were published by the National Magazine Company. This company was founded in 1910 by the American newspaper magnate William Randolph Hearst to publish a new Sunday newspaper *The London Budget*, which was produced on American lines with separate magazine and comic sections. The paper was too far ahead of its time to be a success and ceased publication in 1913. In the meantime the company had acquired *Nash's Magazine* in 1911, which it now continued to publish with considerable success. In 1914 they bought *Pall Mall Magazine* from Iliffe & Co., intending to publish it alongside *Nash's Magazine*, but the onset of war and consequent shortage of paper caused the two titles to be merged in a single magazine. In 1922 the company started to publish *Good Housekeeping*, a title that was already a success in America for Hearst's International Magazine Company. To facilitate the use of American material in the magazine it was printed in a larger format than was usual for British magazines, having a page size of 294×217 mm compared with the 245×165 mm that had been common to *Nash's Magazine*, *Pall Mall Magazine* and their competitors since the 1890s. The following year *Nash's Pall Mall Magazine* was enlarged to the same format. From November 1925 both magazines were printed on a new Cotterell rotary press with two sets of cylinders allowing illustrations to be printed in black and white and one colour.

At the time that Heath Robinson had moved to Cranleigh his brother Charles was living in Crouch Hall Road, Crouch End. Two neighbours there, and friends of the younger generation of Robinsons, had attended Highgate school where they had made friends with Alan McPeake and all three were regular visitors to the Robinson household for Saturday evening entertainments around the piano. Alan's father, J. Y. McPeake, was the man that Randolph Hearst had sent to England from Ireland in 1910 to edit *The London Budget*. When that paper failed he stayed on as a director of the National Magazine Company and in 1919 was made Managing Director. His son Alan started his career in publishing that year with *The Westminster Gazette* and in 1923 became art editor of both *Nash's Pall Mall Magazine* and *Good Housekeeping*. Thus there were ties of friendship between the Robinsons and the National Magazine

Company, which perhaps explains why they were the only publishers to commission serious illustrations from Heath Robinson during the 1920s and 1930s.

His first such illustration for the company was a pen and wash drawing to a story by Clemence Dane called 'Spinsters Rest' that appeared in *Nash's Pall Mall Magazine* in September 1925. The starting point for the story was an extract from one of Grimm's fairy tales, and the double page illustration of an old woman sitting in front of a large fireplace with the ethereal figures of her dreams parading in front of her derives much from Heath Robinson's fantasy illustrations of ten years earlier. His next illustration for the company, published some eighteen months later, was also a double page headpiece to a Clemence Dane piece, this time in *Good Housekeeping*. The article, called 'A Sex of Queens', had as its subject the tragedy of marriage that is spiritually broken, and the unlikely theme that Heath Robinson was asked to illustrate was 'A Suggested Brooming-out of Modern Social Life'. This gave him the

'But God would not let him die.'
Illustration from 'The Witch Girl',
Nash's Pall Mall Magazine, 1929)

'"There were three little boys who threw stones at me, and a gamekeeper and an old farm labourer who laughed," said Simon.' Illustration from 'I'll Tell You Everything', *Nash's Pall Mall Magazine*, 1932.

opportunity to draw on a strong element of fantasy once again for an excellent illustration showing women and young girls, all wearing crowns, sweeping and washing away hideous little goblins and demons.

The circulation figures for *Nash's Pall Mall Magazine* had been declining since the war and in order to increase the company's share of the market it was decided to start a new magazine. In May 1927 *Pall Mall* was launched again as a separate publication from *Nash's Magazine*. Initially it had a smaller page size, was unillustrated and published only fiction. However after its first year in this form the new venture showed no sign of breaking

even and the company decided to change it into a general interest
illustrated magazine with a format very similar to *Nash's Magazine*. In
order to cope with the increased requirement for illustrations that this
change created, more staff had to be employed and Heath Robinson's
eldest son, Oliver, joined the company as an assistant art editor in April
1928. He took over most of the work on *Good Housekeeping*, allowing
Alan McPeake to concentrate on the launch of the new illustrated *Pall
Mall*, the first issue of which appeared in August 1928. The new magazine
was so similar to *Nash's Magazine* that with the names covered one
would find it almost impossible to tell them apart and a market that
would barely support one *Nash's Magazine* certainly could not support
two. In May 1929 the two titles were re-amalgamated, the company
having suffered heavy losses. At this time, and for the rest of its life, it was
only the substantial profits from *Good Housekeeping* that enabled *Nash's
Pall Mall Magazine* to continue in print.

Heath Robinson made two 'serious' contributions to the new *Pall Mall*
before its demise. The first was an atmospheric pen and wash drawing in
the 1928 Christmas number showing people in Victorian dress making
their way through an old-fashioned, snow-covered town centre to church.
It illustrated an article by A. S. Peake called 'What is the Danger of
Christmas?' This was followed by a full colour cover for the 1928 New
Year number, a whimsical and decorative design showing a number of
people in the court dress of Charles I playing croquet in a formal garden.
This was a style of painting he was to develop over the next fifteen years,
especially in the large coloured plates he produced for *Holly Leaves*
which was the title given to the Christmas number of the *Illustrated
Sporting and Dramatic News*. The subjects for these large and complex
compositions were celebrations or occasions involving large gatherings of
people enjoying themselves. The first to be published was 'The Fair Day'
which, whilst exhibiting complexity of composition and colouring is
still closely linked to his cartoon drawings in the treatment of figures.
During the 1930s he continued to develop the style and probably the best
is 'The Toast' published in 1935. Looking at this picture one is reminded
of Breughel's paintings, and in particular of one of the most perfect of that
artist's human comedies, the famous picture of 'A Country Wedding'.
Both artists display a mastery of composition in organizing their pictures
in a way that does not look crowded or confusing. Heath Robinson was
very proud of these paintings and referring to one called 'The Christening
Party' which Langston Day reproduced in his biography in 1947, told
a friend that he would rather sell his clothes than part with it.

In the Christmas issue of *Nash's Magazine* for 1928 was a new poem
by Laurence Housman called 'Hop-O'-Me-Heart' for which Heath

'Pianella's cab was disappearing in the distance.'
Illustration from 'I'll Tell You Everything', *Nash's Pall Mall Magazine*, 1932

Robinson made four full page illustrations. These were executed in pen
and ink with grey and either green or pink washes and each was a series of
linked illustrations and decorations that forms a frame around the verse on
the centre of the page. In the best of them Heath Robinson probably
came closer than he would ever again to recapturing the magic of *The
Strand Magazine* fairytale illustrations.

His largest and most important commission from the National
Magazine Company came at the end of 1931 when he was asked to
provide illustrations to a novel jointly written by J.B. Priestley and
Gerald Bullett called 'I'll Tell You Everything'. This was serialised in
nine parts in *Nash's Pall Mall Magazine* between March and November
1932 and for it Heath Robinson made nineteen large pen and wash
illustrations and one small line drawing. As with all Heath Robinson's
work for this magazine, the original drawings are large, seventeen of
them extending across two boards, each about 500mm tall by 300mm
wide. A single colour was used in addition to black and white in four of

the drawings and it is interesting to note that one of the illustrations originally executed in red, black and white was printed in green, black and white in the magazine, losing some of its visual impact, but presumably fitting in better with whatever else was printed on the same sheet as it came off the press. The drawings show a wide range of effects expressed within a consistent style, from the dramatic to the farcical. In the illustration in which the hero is being locked in a lumber room by a sinister old man every piece of junk stands out with great clarity, forming a complex mosaic between the two characters. In the succeeding drawing variety of texture is achieved by drawing the barn and trees in the background in soft pencil, making the sharply drawn figures stand out even more clearly. The scenes of the car chase and of the policeman catching the small boys bring out the humorous side of the story, whilst the picture in the final part of the hero galloping down stairs brandishing a musket and a sabre is full of dramatic action. The whole sequence is a fine example of sustained illustration in a style that was being developed by Heath Robinson, L. G. Illingworth and one or two other artists almost exclusively for publication in magazines such as *Nash's Pall Mall Magazine* and *The Strand Magazine*.

During the period between the wars magazine illustration was a disciplined and a demanding occupation. Generally an editor would pass an author's text to the art editor about three months before it was due to be published. Of this period the artist was allowed about three weeks to complete his work, the remainder of the time being taken up in making

'"They laugh at you, you warns them again, they throw stones, so what do you do?"'

blocks, preparing the work for the printer, printing and distribution, in many cases world wide. Usually the art editor would choose the subjects to be illustrated, having regard to the relationship between pictures and text, and ensuring that the reader was attracted without giving away too much of the plot. The art editor also decided how much of the double page spread was available for illustration and whether colour was to be used. The artist was then required to make roughs for approval by the art editor and to be used in planning the overall layout of the pages. Once they were approved he could then go on to prepare the finished drawings. In his book *Magazine Illustration* published in 1939, George Leech R.I., for many years art editor of *The Strand Magazine*, identified three main principles of magazine illustration. These were that the pictures should illustrate the author's text, that they should decorate the page and that they should reproduce well. He also wrote:

> One or two of the well known illustrators
> are sufficiently versatile to tackle almost any
> kind of story, but the majority are only
> really good when dealing with the type
> that appeals specially to them.

In his work for *Nash's Pall Mall Magazine* and *Good Housekeeping* Heath Robinson rarely failed to achieve all three of Leech's

"I takes 'em in charge," says Dumble, "and puts 'em in my notebook."'
Illustration from 'I'll Tell You Everything', *Nash's Pall Mall Magazine*, 1932

principles and without doubt proved himself capable of illustrating a very wide range of stories and articles.

Amongst the many other serious illustrations he produced for the two magazines between 1933 and 1938 two sets stand out both because of the quality of the pictures and of the stories they illustrate. The first is 'The Man Who Could Work Miracles', a long story by H. G. Wells that appeared in *Nash's Pall Mall Magazine* in January 1936. The other is A. J. Cronin's short story 'Mascot for Uncle' that appeared in the same magazine in December 1936.

'"Get out of the way," Simon blazed at him,
tightening his grasp on the sword and the pistol.'
Illustration from 'I'll Tell You Everything',
Nash's Pall Mall Magazine, 1932

It must not be thought that all of Heath Robinson's work for the National Magazine Company was of a serious kind. Over the years they used his humorous drawings in greater numbers. The majority of these commissions were out of the ordinary, calling for illustrations to fit in with a text, often in halftone and sometimes using one colour as well as black and white. So even these must have provided some respite from the constant need to think up new ideas for the familiar full page cartoons that most other magazines were asking for.

Heath Robinson's first job for the company had been to illustrate four humorous essays by Stephen Leacock in 1921 for *Nash's Pall Mall Magazine*, which was still being published in its smaller format. These drawings are in the style that he was then using for his cartoons, which at that time was at its least refined and at its closest to extreme caricature. The figures are stiff and shapeless, seemingly made from beach balls with arms and legs attached, and the long nosed men invariably appear to be prancing around on tip-toe. Following these somewhat strange illustrations he was asked to illustrate one more piece by the same writer called 'How I Raised My Own Salary.' It was published in December 1925, and by this time his style had become much more refined and he was approaching his peak as a humorous illustrator. The article was one of the main attractions in the Christmas number of *Nash's Pall Mall Magazine* and for it Heath Robinson supplied ten small two-colour half-tone drawings.

The following March he provided five pen and wash drawings to illustrate an article by Frank Swinnerton in *Nash's Pall Mall Magazine* entitled 'On Giving Way to Things'. These are typical of his best humorous work. The fine pen lines are perfectly controlled and whilst foreground objects such as Mr. Marigold's loaded breakfast table are drawn in great detail, a single shadow is used to suggest the presence of a wall, or a hat and gloves resting on it, a floor. Each of the drawings, framed only by the surrounding text, is an object lesson in composition. The subject matter is the frailty and foibles of human beings and here we find the direct successors to the rustic drawings of *A Midsummer Night's Dream*.

Frank Swinnerton was both an old friend and a close neighbour. The two had first met in the days when the three Robinson brothers were hawking their drawings around the publishers offices of London. At that time Swinnerton was occupying a desk in the outer office of J. M. Dent and Heath Robinson said that it was encouraging to meet one so friendly in the enemy's camp at those anxious moments. In the early 1920s Swinnerton moved to Cranleigh, occupying 'Old Tokefield', the house that had previously belonged to Lawson Wood. By March 1925 Heath

Robinson had already provided one double page drawing to a Frank Swinnerton article and over the next four years he illustrated thirteen more, mostly in *Good Housekeeping*. Their partnership came to an end in November 1929 when Frank Swinnerton was appointed book critic of the *Evening News*. Heath Robinson continued to provide humorous drawings for *Nash's Pall Mall Mgazine* and *Good Housekeeping* until Christmas 1934, illustrating articles by such well known writers as Harold Nicholson, J.B. Priestley and Beverley Nichols, but none quite reached the high standards set during his collaboration with Swinnerton.

Heath Robinson's cover design for the 1929 New Year issue of *Pall Mall Magazine* has already been mentioned. Possibly the most striking pictures that he made for the National Magazine Company were the other cover designs by him for the Christmas numbers of either *Nash's Pall Mall Magazine* or *Good Housekeeping* between 1924 and 1929. One of the best was the picture of a pedlar for *Nash's Pall Mall Magazine* in 1929 that John Lewis used on the dustwrapper of his book on Heath Robinson in 1972. The earliest of these designs, for *Good Housekeeping* in 1924, was also featured on the dustwrapper of a book published in 1925 entitled *The Good Housekeeping Cookery Book*. This design shows a young girl rolling out pastry, helped in her work by six of the little goblins that were to feature in many of the designs. These covers with their sharply drawn figures, bright warm colours, and liberal use of gold must have done much to brighten the bookstalls at Christmas time. During the 1920s the covers of *Nash's Pall Mall Magazine* were normally the preserve of Harrison Fisher with his fashionable paintings of girl's heads, whilst those of *Good Housekeeping* were usually designed by Jessie Wilcox Smith, and so for any other artist to be asked to design a cover for either magazine was something of an honour.

Whilst the National Magazine Company seems to have had a monopoly of Heath Robinson as a serious illustrator between the wars, his humorous illustrations were occasionally seen in the pages of their competitors. To Londoners in the 1920s the word farce was synonymous with Ben Travers' plays at the Aldwych Theatre. The first and one of the most successful was 'A Cuckoo in the Nest', staged in 1925. That same year *The Passing Show*, a popular weekly magazine, published a series of twelve humorous pieces by him. Six came out under the collective title 'Old Tales Retold' and the remainder as 'Misguided Lives'. In each case a well known story such as 'Beauty and the Beast' or the name of a character such as 'Hamlet' was taken as the starting point for an amusing and unfamiliar version of the original tale, much of which was told in contemporary slang. In every story about a third of the double page spread given over to the tale was filled by an illustration by W. Heath Robinson. These illustrations make an interesting contrast with his humorous illustrations for *Nash's Pall Mall Magazine* and *Good Housekeeping*. In them he has adapted his style to suit both the coarser wit of Ben Travers and the poorer quality paper and printing style of the magazine, which precluded the use of halftone plates. The illustrations are drawn with broad, open lines and the originals look somewhat crude, but the reduced pictures look well on the printed page and perfectly reflect the comedy of the text. Following the success of 'A Cuckoo in the Nest' Travers was no longer a regular contributor to *The Passing Show* but he wrote a few more pieces in the same style for special Christmas or Summer numbers. These too were illustrated by Heath Robinson, who also provided drawings for a similar adult fairy tale by A. A. Thomson and to an article entitled 'Beds' by Groucho Marx published in 1931.

4

Goblins and Gadgets

It was in 1929, ten years after arriving in Cranleigh that Heath Robinson moved again, this time back to the area of North London that he had left twenty years earlier. His daughter Joan had left home to train as a nurse, whilst his eldest son Oliver was working for *Good Housekeeping* whose offices were in Queen Victoria Street in the City of London. The other children were nearing the end of their schooling, and would in all probability find jobs in London also, and so the family home was established in Highgate, first in Shepherd's Hill and then from 1934 at 25 Southwood Avenue, the house in which Heath Robinson was to spend the remaining years of his life. It was hard to leave the country life and the friends they had made in Cranleigh but there were compensations. His brother Charles was still living in Crouch Hall Road, Crouch End, which was within walking distance, as were the Holloway Road and Highgate Hill, scenes of many childhood adventures, and Hampstead Heath where he had first tried to earn his living as a landscape painter.

At this time Heath Robinson's fame as 'The Gadget King' was growing and in 1930, along with the general run of advertising and magazine work, came an unusual commission. He was engaged by the Canadian Pacific Railway Company to decorate the children's room and cocktail bar of their newest and largest transatlantic liner, 'The Empress of Britain', which was being built in Scotland. The commission pleased him greatly and he said that he was honoured to be associated with the many other famous artists involved in the decoration of the ship. Among them were such well known names as Frank Brangwyn, Edmund Dulac and Maurice Greiffenhagen. His designs were painted on large wooden panels at his studio in Highgate, where his son Alan was allowed to help with some of the work. They were transported to the shipyards of John Brown on the Clyde to be installed and Heath Robinson then spent four days on board to put the finishing touches to his work. As well as wall and ceiling panels he also designed a service of china for use in the children's room which was made by W. R. Midwinter of Burslem. Around the tops of the taller pieces and the borders of the plates, ran a frieze of children's faces, whilst the main decorations, in the centre of the plates and on the sides of the other pieces, were illustrations to nursery rhymes with the accompanying verses. These decorations were applied in full colour and many of the

86

nursery rhyme illustrations include the familiar Heath Robinson goblins that had been a feature of his more whimsical work for many years and were soon to have a volume devoted to them. The ship was used as a troop carrier during the second world war and was sunk by a German submarine, and so all that remains of the children's room today are some pieces of china. Fortunately the designs for the cocktail bar are preserved in more complete form for they were published by *The Strand Magazine* in December 1931 with a humorous commentary by Anthony Armstrong, and the article also includes a photograph of the finished bar, which was known as the 'Knickerbocker Bar'. Among the designs are a number of circular panels, including some particularly imaginative ones for the ceiling, which must have made drinkers who had had one cocktail too many wonder quite where they were!

Another unusual commission for Heath Robinson came when he was asked to make a contribution to the British Hospitals air pageant which was to tour the country during the summer of 1933. He responded by creating a fierce Chinese dragon. The advance publicity for the show announced that:

This strange multi-coloured monster of the air whose features have

Heath Robinson decorating the BAC Drone for the Hospitals' Air Pageant

been designed and painted by the famous comic artist specially for the air pageant, is a remarkable BAC Drone aeroplane, driven by a six-horsepower engine — the smallest engine ever used in aviation.

This machine was known at the time as the flying motorcycle. It cruised at 50mph and could land at 20mph. The public were promised that at the pageant

> ... Mr. J. C. Langmore, the well known glider pilot, will demonstrate his complete control over Mr. Heath Robinson's gigantic winged reptile. He will make it twist and turn a few feet above the ground, hop over hedges, glide between trees, then soar to a thousand feet and then swoop on the pageant ground to attack St. George.

It must have been an awesome sight!

Around the end of 1932 Heath Robinson received his first request for nine years to return to book illustration, although in this case the drawings were to have much more in common with his contemporary cartoon work than with his earlier book illustrations. The request came from John Lane and was for a coloured frontispiece and a number of line drawings to illustrate a book called *The Incredible Adventures of Professor Branestawm* written by Norman Hunter. This was a children's story telling, as the title suggests, of the adventures of the archetypal absent minded inventor. The professor himself provides an ideal subject for Heath Robinson, with his bald head on which he kept five pairs of spectacles, whilst the professor's inventions give the artist endless scope to devise the eccentric mechanical devices for which he was already well known. This was the first time that Heath Robinson had illustrated a book in his cartoon style and it works very well. The illustration showing the professor's entry into North Pagwell library on a home made penny-farthing is a masterpiece, with books, furniture and librarian all flying in different directions and the great wheel of the bicycle at the centre of the drawing forming the axis about which everything else is moving.

The book was published for Christmas 1933 and appeared in a large octavo format in bright orange boards. It seems not to have sold very well, only gaining popularity after the second world war when a paperback edition was published by Penguin Books, and now the first edition is quite scarce. Since the first Penguin edition was issued in 1946 it has been reprinted about twenty times and in 1965 a new hard-covered edition was published by The Bodley Head. This too has been reprinted many times, so the book now seems to be more popular than it ever was. Unfortunately though, neither the paperback nor the more recent hard-covered editions reproduce the original coloured frontispiece. Indeed, the publishers seem to have forgotten that it ever existed and in recent years have

'And went whizzing straight inside.'
The Incredible Adventures of Professor Branestawm
(John Lane The Bodley Head, 1933)

gone to the trouble of colouring one of the line drawings to serve as a
wrapper design, ignoring Heath Robinson's wonderful depiction of the
professor flying high above the countryside in his home-made aeroplane,
which would have served their purposes far better.

Undoubtedly, by 1933, Heath Robinson was best known for his
cartoons, but people also knew him as the creator of a strange family of

fairy folk and goblins. These characters appeared first as part of Titania's retinue in *A Midsummer Night's Dream*, and soon re-appeared in one of the illustrations for 'The Rusty Pot and the Wooden Balls' in *The Strand Magazine* in 1916. The same year Heath Robinson designed the cover for Walter Carroll's piano music, *Forest Fantasies*, in which one of the goblins features playing the bagpipes as he leads a fairy procession through the trees. Then in 1919 *The Graphic* Christmas number published a full page coloured illustration to eight lines of verse entitled 'The Little Folk' which showed a procession of Heath Robinson goblins playing musical instruments and coming over a hill top. A similar picture was published the following year, this time to ten lines of verse entitled 'The Old "Visiters"', showing another procession of the goblin folk marching through the snow to bring food to a poor girl in her cottage. There were similar pictures in subsequent Christmas Numbers and at Christmas 1924 the goblins were to be found helping out in the kitchen on the cover of *Good Housekeeping*. They featured on another *Good Housekeeping* cover at Christmas 1928 and on the cover of *Nash's Pall Mall Magazine* for Christmas 1929 where they appeared as the customers of the fairy's pedlar.

As has already been mentioned, in 1916 Heath Robinson illustrated 'The Rusty Pot and the Wooden Balls' in *The Strand Magazine*. This story was taken from Vernaleken's collection of Bohemian folk-tales, *In the Land of Marvels*. Although Constable had rejected this title in favour of *Perrault's Fairy Tales* when chosing a successor to *Peacock Pie*, he did not give up the idea of illustrating the book. In June 1922 he left with A. E. Johnson three pen drawings illustrating the stories 'The Wild Cat of the forest', 'The Fairest Bride' and 'The Three Wondrous Fishes', all from *In the Land of Marvels*. Presumably he wanted Johnson to show them to various publishers in the hope of getting a contract to illustrate a new edition, but he had no success and it was not until 1933 that he was finally able to start work on the book for Hutchinson. It was published in 1934 under the title *Heath Robinson's Book of Goblins* and contained 7 coloured plates, 8 full page and 45 smaller line drawings and 93 vignettes depicting the eponymous goblins. The change of title was obviously an attempt by the publisher to cash in both on Heath Robinson's reputation as a humorist and on the popularity of his already well known goblin pictures, and the vignettes are far and away the best things in the book. It was unfortunate that Constable did not give the artist the opportunity to illustrate the book fifteen years earlier, for the 1916 *Strand Magazine* pictures show what might have been whilst the 1933 book only shows how much Heath Robinson's vigour and power as an illustrator of fantasy had declined. The larger drawings in the book are stiff, coarse and totally

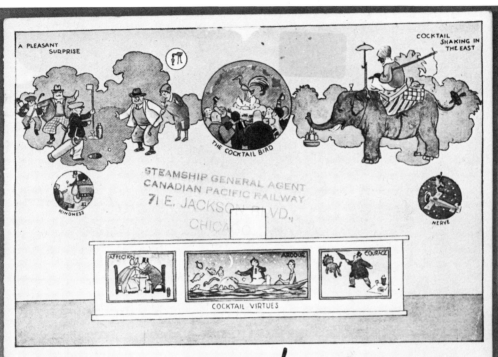

Front cover of a twelve-page advertising booklet
issued by Canadian Pacific

'Girl on a Slope.' One of the watercolours that W. Heath
Robinson painted for his own enjoyment.
Previously unpublished

lacking in drama compared with the earlier work and the coloured plates, although possessing a certain charm, seem clumsy compared with the delicate and rhythmic compositions of *Hans Andersen* or *A Midsummer Night's Dream*.

It was published as a thick quarto with a blue morocco grained cloth binding blocked in imitation gold which soon tarnished. There was also a rather gaudy *de luxe* edition in green imitation leather with rounded

A vignette from *Heath Robinson's Book of Goblins*
(Hutchinson & Co. Ltd., 1934)

corners and gilded edges. The book has never been republished, but in 1978 Hutchinson brought out a delightful little volume called *Goblins* in which a number of the goblin vignettes were enlarged and coloured and each given an accompanying verse written by Spike Milligan. The final product was one of which the artist would surely have approved, had he ever seen it.

Young readers of *Heath Robinson's Book of Goblins* might well have been

pleasantly surprised to find pictures by the same artist decorating one of
their school books. Writing of his own school days Heath Robinson said:

> My head was never worried with foreign or dead languages, which
> perhaps was good for it at that time of mental confusion.

So no doubt he called on one or other of his children for help when asked
to illustrate *Balbus* by G.M. Lyne. This describes itself as 'A Latin
Reading Book for Junior Forms' and in it the author has attempted to
hold the interest of his twelve- or thirteen-year-old readers by intro-
ducing a little humour into a series of short stories in Latin. If it were not
for their unusual context the full page drawings in the book would have
little interest for the collector today, but the two small vignettes are
somewhat different in style, suggesting perhaps that Heath Robinson
had taken note of the work of Walt Disney, and even tried his hand at
something similar. This book is now, by its nature, quite hard to find, but
then how many secondhand booksellers inspect Latin primers closely
enough to recognise such a rarity when it comes their way?

To Heath Robinson the year of 1934 was memorable because it saw
the creation at the 'Ideal Home Exhibition' at Olympia of his ideal home,
'The Gadgets'. The house stood on a site 50 ft by 30 ft and was nearly
20 ft high. It was peopled with more than thirty life-like moving figures,
all busy about their daily tasks. Father, mother, baby, nurse — each was
modelled by the engineering firm of Veranco Ltd, under the supervision
of their creator, to a scale of half life-size. Each too was said to be fitted
for clothes of a fashionable kind, although to whose idea of fashion is not
quite clear. The visitor could see the family in action from the time they
were woken in the morning until they retired at night. Father and mother
dropping through the bedroom floor to the dining room beneath on the
end of counter-balanced ropes would by so doing turn on the radio-
gramophone, give the cat its milk and uncover the breakfast sausages.

A special correspondent writing in the *Daily Mail* described the scene
thus:

> The Mangle-lady mangled — and mangled — and the clothes went
> out of the window in an endless stream, past the carrot trees and
> Spuderia, the potato bush, and over the back of the cow that cropped
> the never growing lawn, till they reached the clothes post at the end of
> the vegetable orchard — and then they ran down the posts into the
> baskets.
>
> Out from an attic window with crooked shutters set in the crumpled
> roof popped Mrs Miffin, a servant, to throw a flirtatious glance at
> Mr. Twilp a manservant.
>
> Mr. Twilp had just leaned out of a window below to throw a glad
> eye up at her — but he had gone in again.

Life is just like that!

But Twilp and Miffin keep on trying to exchange smiles.

Then Leonard the powerhouseman started up. His the energy that powers the house! He pedalled and pedalled.

He pedalled out electricity by running a dynamo and simultaneously pedalled hot-water jugs and bottles, scuttles of coal and cups of tea in a weird procession to an upstairs window.

.. and so on.

One can only speculate on what might remain of this fabulous creation —a few newspaper reports certainly, and it is rumoured that a set of postcards depicting 'The Gadgets' was sold at the exhibition. It also seems likely that somewhere in a film archive there might be some newsreel footage showing Heath Robinson's creation in action. He was now indeed the gadget king!

Between 1926 and 1929 Heath Robinson had produced some of his best humorous illustrations to accompany articles by Frank Swinnerton in *Good Housekeeping*. However, during the 1930s Swinnerton moved on to more serious forms of writing, and although Heath Robinson continued to do similar work with a variety of authors, it was not until 1935 that he found a new partner for this light-hearted form of illustration. It is fitting that this new partnership should have been inaugurated between the covers of *The Strand Magazine*, which had commissioned work from him in a variety of styles since 1908. In 1935 *The Strand Magazine* was still maintaining its high standards of illustration and the November issue, featuring such artists as Arthur Wragg, Will Owen and L. G. Illingworth, also included an article entitled 'At Home with Heath Robinson'. This had a text by Kenneth R. G. Browne and ten pen and wash illustrations by Heath Robinson. The illustrations, which showed novel uses for unwanted items, were drawn under the title 'Rejuvenated Junk', and the series originally included three more drawings of which 'The Converted Egg-Whisk' and 'The Pipe Knocker' are two. The latter drawing is actually mentioned in the article, although room could not be found to reproduce it, and it is probable that the drawings preceded the text.

K. R. G. Browne, a fellow 'Savage', was an ideal collaborator for Heath Robinson. He was the son of Gordon Browne who is still well known as an illustrator of books and magazines, and was the grandson of Hablot Knight Browne, who under his pen name of 'Phiz' gained lasting fame as the illustrator of many Victorian novelists, including Charles Dickens, Charles Lever and Harrison Ainsworth. The article in *The Strand Magazine* marked the start of a partnership that was only brought to an untimely end by the death of Kenneth Browne in 1940. Heath Robinson wrote of the books and articles they produced together:

'The Pipe Knocker'
(Previously unpublished)

'The Converted Egg Whisk'
(Previously unpublished)

This collaboration seems to have solved a difficulty that I have often found with my lighter drawings. They rarely lend themselves to illustration in the ordinary sense of the term. It is the equal partnership in our mutual productions which is so satisfactory, at least to me. Instead of the finished story being handed to the artist to illustrate, we start level. Before we begin our different parts, we discuss the matter between us. In this way each is able to help the other. A consistency between the artist's and the writer's work is secured which cannot easily be obtained in any other way. My partner in these undertakings has a delightful sense of humour. It is great fun devising with him these little plots to make our readers laugh at themselves and one another.

During 1932 and 1933 Heath Robinson had drawn a series of cartoons for *The Sketch* entitled 'Flat Life', which depicted various gadgets designed to make the most of the limited space available in the contemporary flat. It was this series of drawings that provided K. R. G. Browne and W. Heath Robinson with the inspiration for their first full length book together. It was called *How to Live in a Flat*, and as well as greatly extending the original ideas showing many ingenious ways of overcoming the problems caused by lack of space in flats and bungalows, also provided much fun at the expense of the more extreme designs in thirties furniture and architecture. There is an extended section which explores the possibilities of tubular steel furniture, including a chair with a tap on the side providing a continuous supply of beer through the tubular frame from a barrel in the basement below. Geometric carpet designs, many of which

    ... appear to have been designed by colour-blind surrealists under the influence of some potent drug ...

were made more practical in the 'Heath Robinson Games Rug' which can be used for chess, draughts and halma. Architectural designs were also gently satirised with curved windows and balconies much in evidence throughout.

The book was published by Hutchinson for Christmas 1936 and was well received. Over the next three years K. R. G. Browne and Heath Robinson successfully repeated the formula with *How to be a Perfect Husband, How to make a Garden Grow* and *How to be a Motorist*. Heath Robinson received much teasing from his family about the choice of subject for the second book, *How to be a Perfect Husband*, but looking back over his cartoons one finds that romance and courtship had been amongst his most frequently chosen subjects, from the early 'Cupid' cartoons to such pictures as 'The Coquette' and 'Stolen Kisses' which were reproduced in *Absurdities* in 1934.

It is a popular misconception that Heath Robinson's work appeared regularly in the pages of *Punch*. In fact, apart from one cartoon in the Summer number for 1923, his only contributions were seven of his drawings for the *How to . . .* books. The first four, which appeared in the latter half of 1936, were from the drawings prepared for *How to Live in a*

'Modern carpet designs may provide endless entertainment for your friends.'
How to Live in a Flat (Hutchinson & Co. Ltd., 1936)

Flat, although only two of the four were used in the book. Then, in the Spring of 1937, three of the drawings that had been made for *How to be a Perfect Husband* were also published in *Punch*, of which two were later used in the book. These were the last of his pictures to be published in *Punch*, but the next *How to . . .* book received a more complete preview when *The Strand Magazine* published an article called 'A Highly Complicated Science' in August 1938. The science referred to was that of gardening and the article by K.R.G. Browne was accompanied by nine of Heath Robinson's drawings all of which were subsequently used in *How to Make a Garden Grow*. The captions to the drawings were changed for the book, many being shortened. For example, 'The curvilinear re-entrant snuff-spray prevents spraying the people next door' was changed to 'The Re-Entrant Snuff-Spray'.

Much of the subject matter for this book and the next, *How to be a Motorist* (1939), was drawn from Heath Robinson's earlier cartoons. Amongst his earliest work for the *Sketch* was a series of drawings on the practicalities of gardening, including a picture of 'root pruning' showing the gardener tunnelling down to the roots of a plant to prune them, and although the earlier drawing is much more elaborate, the idea is the same as is presented on page 27 of *How to Make a Garden Grow*. Similarly the theme of motoring recurs frequently in the earlier cartoons, with the three sets of motoring cartoons in *Out and Away* 1919-1920, *The Home Made Car* series which first appeared in *The Strand Magazine* in 1921 and *Motor Mania*, a book of cartoons which was published by *The Motor Owner* magazine the same year, being amongst the best of them.

But there is an important difference between the full page cartoon and the humorous book. The cartoon must be capable of making the reader laugh whatever his mood as he turns the page and so must achieve an instant impact with a strong idea and sound execution. The reader of a humorous book, on the other hand, will have picked it up in the expectation of being amused, and so here the author or artist's problem is one of how to sustain the humour in an extended form, rather than to create a sudden effect with a single idea. In the *How to . . .* books Heath Robinson found the opportunity to present the reader with a set of variations on a theme, allowing him to look at his subject from every angle and to explore each idea that presented itself. Thus the books allow us to see a different aspect of his humorous art; to see its depth, rather than just selected high points.

On the 5th April 1940 Kenneth Browne died at the age of 45, but fortunately this did not mean that the series of *How to . . .* books had come to an end. The onset of the second world war provided new and topical subject matter, and Heath Robinson found a writer amongst his neighbours in Highgate. This was Cecil Hunt, who at 38 had already had published a number of humorous books, as well as standard works on journalism and short story writing, books of literary reminiscences and a variety of books on other subjects. He had been fiction editor of the *Daily Mail* and the *Evening News*, literary editor of the *Daily Mail* and was also a regular broadcaster. In 1940 he was perhaps best known for his series of 'Howler' books, the most recent of which had been *Hand-Picked Howlers* published in 1937 with illustrations by Edmund Blampied. Three titles resulted from the new partnership, *How to Make the Best of Things, How to Build a New World* and *How to Run a Communal Home*.

Another of Cecil Hunt's earlier titles had been *Author-Biography* and perhaps Heath Robinson had read this before starting to write his own autobiography in 1937. This was commissioned by Blackie & Son, the Glasgow publisher, and like most autobiographies by people who are not professional writers, must have seemed something of a gamble to them even with the prospect of Heath Robinson's drawings, both new and old, to brighten the book and provide added interest. They need not have worried, for the book that Heath Robinson wrote was a true reflection of the man and a rare example of the best kind of autobiography. He wrote with honesty, naturalness of style, modesty and an obvious affection for his fellow men. Kenneth Browne wrote to him after reading the book:

> ... I think you have made an extremely good job of it. One would think you had been a professional writer all your days, in fact.

The reviewer in *John O' London's Weekly* summed up the qualities of the book when he said:

> He writes seriously — which is not to say dully — and quietly about his heritage and his upbringing, and his business, his taste and his good fortune. He is human, not humorous, straightforward and not whim-sical; and since his life has hardly been one of action, this is a book which depends more on its humanity than any other quality.

Reading through the contemporary reviews one finds that the book was universally well received and recommended, a reception that seems to have been reserved for a relatively small proportion of books published at that time. It is amusing to note in many of the reviews an air of surprise, firstly that Heath Robinson was a real person and secondly that he was, in his everyday life, a normal and sane family man. One feels that some reviewers were disappointed not to receive a piece of knotted string and a set of plans for a page-turning machine with their copy of the book.

Its publication made Heath Robinson something of a literary celebrity, at least for a short period. He was invited to lecture at the *Sunday Times* National Book Fair where he demonstrated, among other things, how to split peas with an axe! He was also one of the guests at a Foyles literary lunch, along with James Agate, Pamela Frankau, A. G. MacDonnell and others. Billed to speak at the lunch on 'Art', he said that he had always encouraged modern art and would show the Vorticist patent match

THE ENCHANTED ISLE
Violin and Piano

WALTER
CARROLL

W HEATH
ROBINSON

Forsyth Brothers Ltd.

Front cover design for sheet music.
(Forsyth Brothers Ltd., 1946)

extinguisher, which might also be Cubist or Surrealist. He then went to an easel and drew this curious contraption incorporating rubber tubing, a container for compressed air, and a bulb fixed to a post on the floor, by means of which the artist could blow out his match when he had lit his pipe, even when he had a palette in one hand and a brush in the other. Apparently this performance was watched with a silence that no speaker could have commanded.

One result of publishing his autobiography was to put him in contact with people he had worked with many years earlier. In 1941 W.H.D. Rouse, who was then 78 years old, wrote to him:

> The Giant Crab — well I remember my joy in writing that book, and my joy in your pictures, which is as fresh as it was; and when I found in your book that you actually remembered it, and that you felt some joy too, just imagine what a comfort that is to me when the Germans have killed laughter in half the world.

Another old acquaintance with whom he regained contact was the composer Walter Carroll, for whom he had designed two music covers in 1913 and 1916. He wrote to say that he was working on a new collection of pieces for violin and piano for young people and asked whether Heath Robinson would agree to design a cover and title page for the music. When Heath Robinson agreed to make the designs Carroll wrote back:

> First . . . let me tell you the joy your letter gave to me. To know you are well: and to find you are willing to help me in my desire to make my book beautiful to the eye as well as to the ear . . . Of course I am very thrilled at the thought of seeing my story — (or some bits of it) in black and white. I remember now how I tingled when your 'Forest Fantasies' cover arrived. It is as beautiful as ever to me. I never tire of your work.

The drawings were completed in 1943, although wartime restrictions on the use of paper delayed publication until 1946. They must have come up to the composer's expectations, and certainly are among the best line drawings that Heath Robinson published for many years. The collection was called *The Enchanted Isle* and among the pieces it contained was one called 'The Rock Temple'. These two titles taken together inspired Heath Robinson's designs which bear comparison with those for *Forest Fantasies* and *The Countryside* made when the artist was in his prime. Who would guess that such clarity and firmness of line had come from the hand of a seventy-one-year-old artist?

The onset of the second world war in 1939 must have saddened Heath Robinson, filling him with a sense of weariness and futility and he referred to it as 'this disastrous war'. As in the first world war his humorous drawings were much in demand and he was once more given a page in *The Sketch* each week. Comparing the drawings that appeared on that page with those published during the first war, one notices a change of emphasis. During the first war it was the enemy and their behaviour that provided the majority of the subjects for the cartoons. This time most of the jokes feature British soldiers, or even problems on the home front, and one feels that the Nazi enemy was too terrible to be the subject of such a gentle humorist.

During the second world war each side had a single clearly identified politician as leader, and for the first time Heath Robinson produced series of drawings with a living person as their main subject. In *The Sketch* in 1940 appeared a series entitled 'The Ubiquitous Winston' which chronicled the exploits of a Churchill 'super-hero' as he attempts to win the war singlehanded. Adolf Hitler was caricatured in the illustrations to a parody of *Mein Kampf* in doggerel verse by R. F. Patterson entitled *Mein Rant* which was published in 1940 by Blackie & Son. Neither set of illustrations shows Heath Robinson at anything like his best, and he was obviously far more at home when inventing means of reducing discomfort on the home front, for example with the various devices pictured in 'Rational Gadgets for Your Coupons', another series that appeared in *The Sketch* in 1940.

A final echo of Heath Robinson's earlier fantasy illustrations can be found in *Once Upon a Time*, a book of fairy stories written by Dr. Liliane M. C. Clopet and published by Frederick Muller. The four stories in the book gave him a chance to return to many of his favourite subjects. The first story has a young man blown across the sea, as was Vammerdopper in *Uncle Lubin*, and also features a cat. In his later years Heath Robinson's own cat, Saturday Morning, was his constant companion and, as surviving sketch books show, a constant subject for his pencil. The other three stories all feature animals and the reader is treated to a delightful Heath Robinson menagerie including a very robust family of pigs, horses, geese, bears and even ladybirds. There is none of the dramatic tension of his earlier fantasy work, but the drawings are made with a warmth and lively good humour that cannot fail to please. The dustwrapper design, which was printed in black, orange and green, is one of the best of the drawings, full of life and movement and serving as an excellent advertisement for the good things inside.

The author, on receiving the drawings from Muller, wrote back in January 1944:

Thank you very much for sending me on the utterly wonderful illustrations by Mr. Heath Robinson. I didn't know that such a delightful artist existed — or had existed — in the world and I can scarcely believe in my good fortune to have him to do my stories. I like the fun and the sweetness and of course, the sheer beauty of the drawings. I should like — if such a thing were possible — to have one or other of the drawings — signed — to keep, but maybe that is impossible ... what I like so much, as the author, is that the mood of the illustrations is the mood of the stories.

Frontispiece from *Once Upon a Time*
(Frederick Muller Ltd., 1944)

The book was published later in the year in a slim volume that looks more like a book of poetry than a collection of fairy stories. War economy and paper shortage were of course responsible for this meagre format, and for the small number of copies printed, which makes this last book published during Heath Robinson's lifetime one of the scarcest of all his books.

Dr. Clopet asked Heath Robinson to illustrate another book of hers, but by this time he was not a well man and wrote in August 1944:

> I have to go into hospital for an operation, after which I shall need some time to recuperate, so that you see I shall not be able to undertake anything for some little time. Moreover, I have many arrears of work to make up before I undertake anything new.

'She gave him a hot bath.'
Once Upon a Time
(Frederick Muller Ltd., 1944)

He had a preliminary operation and was pronounced fit for a major operation, but on the 13th September 1944, before this took place, he died from heart failure.

Amongst his arrears of work was a new set of illustrations to *Don Quixote* that had been commissioned by Dent for a series of children's

'The boat was gently gliding along.'
The Adventures of Don Quixote de la Mancha
(J. M. Dent & Sons Ltd., 1953)

classics they had in preparation. The series started publication in 1948 under the collective title 'The Children's Illustrated Classics' but it was not until 1953 that the *Don Quixote* appeared. At the time of his death Heath Robinson had completed eight coloured plates and ten line drawings for the book and these the publisher supplemented with a further sixteen black and white illustrations taken from the 1902 edition. This made an uneasy mixture in which the fine flowing lines and vibrant energy of the early drawings contrasts with the thicker outlines, more static compositions and gentle good humour of the later work. That is not to say that the later drawings are less good than those of 1902, merely that they are so different in style as not to appear happily in the same volume. In fact the coloured plates are probably the best book illustrations that Heath Robinson made in the last twenty years of his life.

A memorial exhibition of his work was held at the Fine Art Society in New Bond Street, London in January 1945. It was opened by the cartoonist David Low, and the catalogue had a preface by A. C. R. Carter. Over a hundred pictures were on show and although his humorous ones predominated, there were also serious drawings and watercolours, including the beautiful frontispiece painting for *Bill the Minder*. Visitors to the exhibition, most of whom had previously seen Heath Robinson's work only in reproduction, were struck by the fineness of his craftsmanship, the clean and firm fluency of his pen line and the quality of his water-colour washes.

In 1972 a major exhibition was held at The Medici Gallery in London to mark the centenary of Heath Robinson's birth. The sixty-nine pictures shown presented a well-balanced selection of his work. They included a number of the watercolours he painted for his own amusement as well as a selection of his book illustrations and cartoons, and even one of the illustrations for *Nash's Pall Mall Magazine*. The only noticeable omission was of the early black and white illustrations with no drawings earlier than 1912 in the show.

Heath Robinson's achievements as an artist are best summarised by the reactions on hearing of his death of three people who knew him. In a letter sent to *The Daily Telegraph* on the day that Heath Robinson's obituary had appeared, A. C. R. Carter wrote from his office in Fleet Street:

> I feel it to be just to the memory of Heath Robinson to state that his fame will endure as an imaginative artist of deep powers of interpretation. I remember the stir in artistic circles 44 years ago when the poems of Edgar Allen Poe were illustrated by him in black and white drawings that outrivalled those of Gustav Doré.

The cartoonist Kenneth Bird, better known as 'Fougasse', wrote on the same day:

His work stands for so much for which the rest of us must always be grateful, and especially for that originality in which he was the master of all of us, and the individuality which made it possible. There are few real artists in our branch, and he was such a very real artist in everything he did.

In a letter to the artist's widow, Cecil Hunt wrote that she would:

> ... have the consolation of looking back on a life in which [Heath Robinson] amply fulfilled himself and gave gaiety to untold numbers all over the world. Few men can have had more unseen friends and few led a more thoughtfully happy and gentle spirited life.
>
> I shall always be grateful for the pleasure of knowing him and working with him and seeing from the inside the depth of his mind and the sunny philosophy of his outlook. Glad too that I saw him at work on his serious art which the public, to their loss, so seldom allowed him to offer.
>
> You must be proud and gratified to think how many loved him through his work and how untouched he was by the fame that was rightly his.
>
> There will not be another Heath Robinson; there has never been an imitator which in itself is the highest tribute.

The immediate appeal and general popularity of Heath Robinson during his lifetime resulted mainly from his humorous work and in this field he was both brilliant and unique. He was an unusually prolific artist with a seemingly inexhaustible stock of good ideas. Like artists such as Hogarth and Rowlandson before him, the secret of his appeal lay in his great abilities as a serious artist. His sense of composition and ability to balance mass against mass and to make effective use of large areas of plain white meant that even his most complex cartoons had a unity and rhythm lacking in the work of less talented draughtsmen. Add to this his clarity of line, his ability to adopt strikingly effective novel view points and his innate sense of the decorative effects latent in any design, and one has defined the artistic qualities which, together with his comic genius, have made W. Heath Robinson popular throughout this century.

A Bibliography
of Published Illustrations
by W. Heath Robinson

Notes

This bibliography sets out to list all books, and stories or articles in magazines, published in the United Kingdom up to the end of 1982, that were wholly or partly illustrated by W. Heath Robinson. Editions published outside the United Kingdom are only listed if there was no corresponding United Kingdom edition. It includes all published pictures that were made to illustrate a text whether 'serious' or 'humorous', and also includes a small number of pictures published without an accompanying text in which the subject was 'serious'. In this latter category are the little known series of goblin pictures that appeared in *The Graphic* Christmas issues, *Holly Leaves* and other magazines during the 1920s and the large water-colour pictures that Heath Robinson made for *Holly Leaves*. It does not include books of humorous drawings, cartoons published in periodicals or pictures that were made for use in advertising. Appendix A lists the first publication of books of humorous drawings. Appendix B shows, for a wide range of periodicals, in which years they published either illustrations or cartoons by W. Heath Robinson. The contribution that Heath Robinson made to the world of advertising is a subject in its own right and deserves to have a separate book devoted to it.

ARRANGEMENT
In order to present the reader with a complete picture of the illustrations produced by Heath Robinson at each stage of his career, a single integrated listing has been compiled of the books and magazines in which his illustrations were published. They are listed in chronological order by years of publication of first editions. Within each year books are listed first, followed by magazines.

NUMBERING
Each publication has been given an entry number, and the index refers to entries in the bibliography by this number. Where a book appeared in distinctly different editions, printings or issues, distinguished by more than a change of date on the title page, then each variant is given a letter following the main entry.

TERMINOLOGY
The term 'edition' has been used to refer to all copies of a book printed from the same typesetting and plates. 'Printing' refers to all copies of a book bound from sheets printed at one time. 'Issue' refers to copies of a book bound at the same time and in the same style. Thus there might be several printings of an edition and several issues of a printing.

DATES
When the date of printing of a book appears on the title page or verso, or in a few cases, on the last page of a book, that date is given in the entry following the name of the publisher and place of publication. Otherwise the abbreviation n.d. is used to indicate that the edition was not dated by the publishers. Where a date for the printing or issue can be deduced from publisher's records, advertisements bound into the book, copyright library accession stamps or other reliable source then this date is given in brackets. Less reliable estimates e.g. from inscriptions or prize labels, are given in brackets preceded by the abbreviation 'ca.'

SIZES OF BOOKS
The sizes given for books are page sizes with the page height given first.

DUST WRAPPERS
Details of dustwrappers are given in those instances where they have been seen by the author. However they are extremely ephemeral and the absence of a description of a dustwrapper for a particular book does not mean that there was not one.

RE-USE OF ILLUSTRATIONS
Where illustrations have been re-used with a significantly different text from the one for which they were originally intended, or for an edition in which the contents has been greatly reduced or changed, then the new use is given a separate entry. This is listed in the year in which the altered edition first appeared with a note referring to the first publication of the illustrations.

VOLUME AND PAGE NUMBERS
Most of the periodicals in which Heath Robinson's illustrations appeared were intended by the publishers to be bound into volumes, with each volume comprising issues for between four and twelve months. In many cases bound volumes could be bought from the publishers, or attractive printed cloth cases in which the customer's own copies could be bound were available. For most such periodicals volumes were numbered in sequence. Since most copies of magazines that have survived are in bound volumes, where appropriate a volume number has been given in addition to a date of issue in the entries for magazine illustrations. When trying to correlate dates and volume numbers across a run the researcher should beware of inconsistencies in volume sequences. For example, *Pall Mall Magazine* started with four issues per volume and later changed to six issues per volume, and a change in format resulted in one volume of *The Strand Magazine* having ten issues rather than the usual six.

In most cases periodicals published in volumes were page-numbered by volume rather than by issue, but two exceptions were *Nash's Pall Mall Magazine* and *Good Housekeeping*. From the early 1920s these two magazines also adopted the practice of printing the first few pages of a piece in the front of the magazine and then continuing it towards the back. With very few exceptions the illustrations to such pieces appeared in the front portion of the story or article, and so only those pages are referred to in the relevant entries in the Bibliography.

Chronological Listing

1896

1. 'The Story of Hanna. A Story in Twenty-four Chapters' by W. J. Dawson.
   The Sunday Magazine, Jan-Dec 1896. Vol 25, pp. 8-18, 127-138, 150-161, 268-278, 293-303, 414-420, 480-493, 507-517, 632-641, 655-664, 776-787, 846-856.
   One full page half-tone plate, 38 line drawings and 12 pictorial initials in line.
2. 'The Vision of the Great Spoonbill' by W. H. Hudson.
   The Sunday Magazine, Mar 1896. Vol 25, pp. 198-201.
   Pictorial headpiece and three illustrations in line.
3. 'The Fairy Pedlar'. A poem by Shiela.
   Little Folks, Apr 1896. Vol 43, pp. 256-257.
   One full page line drawing.
4. 'Little Bo Peep'.
   Little Folks, Sep 1896. Vol 44, p. 216.
   One full page line drawing with one colour.

1897

5a. **Danish Fairy Tales and Legends** by Hans Christian Andersen. Bliss, Sands & Co., London, 1897.
   207 × 144 mm. 332 pp. + 20 pp. publisher's catalogue.
   Red morocco grained cloth decorated with illustrations from the book in gilt on front and spine. Titled in gilt on front and spine. Top edge gilt, others uncut.
   16 full page line drawings on coated paper.
   Reprinted, Sands & Co., 1905.

b. A new edition published by Alexander Gardner, Paisley, n.d. (Ca. 1909).
   202 × 144 mm. 332 pp.
   Bound as 5a but with edges trimmed.
   Coloured frontispiece and 15 full page line drawings on coated paper.
   Note: This is a reprint of the Bliss, Sands edition, but with the illustration 'The King's Son...' which faces p. 289 in the first edition coloured, probably by someone other than WHR, and used as the frontispiece. The plate 'The Dustman' which was the frontispiece in the first edition is here inserted facing p. 90. The list of illustrations is reprinted from the first edition and does not reflect these changes.

6a. **The Life and Exploits of the Ingenious Gentleman Don Quixote de la Mancha.** Translated from the original Spanish of Miguel de Cervantes Saavedra by Charles Jarvis Esq. Bliss, Sands & Co., London, 1897.
   224 × 145 mm. xxii, 614 pp. + 2 pp. advertisements.
   Red ribbed cloth titled in gilt on the spine. Edges uncut.
   16 full page line drawings on coated paper.

b. Also issued from 1898 in a more expensive binding of olive green art linen, flat back with headbands, raised gold design and top edge gilt.

c. Reprinted by Sands & Co., 1901. This printing was issued in two different bindings:
   i. The red cloth of the first issue.
   ii. Pale blue cloth printed in black with pictorial designs on the front and spine.

d. Reprinted by Sands & Co., 1902. This printing was issued in three different bindings:
   i. The red cloth of the first issue.

      ii. Green cloth with the pictorial designs of the 1901 printing.

      iii. Royal blue cloth blocked with a design of small flowers, in gilt on the spine and in blind on the front.

  e. Reprinted twice more by Sands & Co., n.d. bound in red cloth, one of the printings on thick paper.

     Note: The pictorial designs used on the bindings of c.ii and d.ii are unsigned, but are probably not by WHR.

7a. **The Pilgrim's Progress from This World to That Which is to Come Delivered Under the Similitude of a Dream** by John Bunyan, edited by George Offor. Bliss, Sands & Co., London 1897.
    224 × 145 mm. xxxii, 284 pp. + 4 pp. advertisements.
    Red ribbed cloth titled in gilt on the spine. Edges uncut.
    Portrait frontispiece from a painting by an unnamed artist and 24 full page line drawings by WHR printed on coated paper.

  b. Also issued from 1898 in a more expensive binding of olive green art linen, flat back with headbands, raised gold design and top edge gilt.

  c. Reprinted by Sands & Co., 1899. This printing was issued in three bindings:
      i. The red cloth of the first issue.
      ii. Pale blue cloth with a pictorial design printed in black on the front and spine.
      iii. Dark red cloth blocked in black with a design of vertical stripes and a pictorial panel on the front showing a monk reading. Titled in gilt on the front and spine.
     Note: This issue had no portrait of Bunyan, and the plate that faced p. 193 in the other issues was here used as the frontispiece. The list of illustrations was not changed to reflect this.

  d. Reprinted by Sands & Co., 1906, bound in royal blue cloth blocked with a design of small flowers.

  e. Reprinted by Drummond's Tract Depot, Stirling and S. W. Partridge, London, n.d. (1908)
    204 × 136 mm. xxxii, 284 pp.
    Beige cloth decorated in brown on the front and spine.

  f. Reprinted by Alexander Gardner, Paisley, n.d.
    201 × 134 mm. xxxii, 284 pp. + 1 p. advertisements.
    Red cloth blocked with pictorial designs from the book on the front and spine, top edge gilt.
    Note: This binding is uniform with those for *Danish Fairy Tales and Legends* and *Tales from Shakespeare* also reprinted by Gardner.

8a. **The Giant Crab and Other Tales from Old India** by W. H. D. Rouse. David Nutt, London, 1897.
    209 × 145 mm. x, 120 pp. + 12 pp. publisher's catalogue.
    Pale blue cloth with a pictorial design printed in navy. Edges uncut.
    Seven full page and 45 smaller line drawings.

  b. Second edition, enlarged, David Nutt, London, 1900.
    209 × 145 mm. x, 134 pp. + 16 pp. publisher's catalogue.
    Beige cloth with the original pictorial design printed in dark brown.
    Illustrations as the first edition.
    Note: This edition contains four additional stories which are not illustrated.

  c. Third edition, The Minerva Press, London, 1973.
    208 × 147 mm. (viii), 112 pp.
    Beige cloth blocked in red with the original pictorial design. Beige or pink dust-wrapper with the binding design repeated.

1898

9a. **The Queen's Story Book**. Being historical stories collected out of English Romantic Literature in illustration of the reigns of English monarchs from the Conquest to Queen Victoria Edited with an introduction by Laurence Gomme.
Archibald Constable & Co., Westminster, 1898.
190 × 125 mm. xvi, 446 pp. + 16 pp. publisher's catalogue.
Royal blue cloth blocked in gilt with an elaborate design of queens and crowns on the front and spine. Top edge gilt, others uncut.
20 full page line drawings on coated paper.

  b. Reprinted 1902 bound in blue cloth printed in red and blocked in gilt with designs of the lion and the unicorn, roses, thistles and shamrocks.

  c. Reprinted n.d. (1904) and 1908 bound in dark blue cloth decorated with acanthus scrolls in green and white and with an oval gilt pictorial panel on the front, titled in gilt on the front and spine. Edges stained green. In the 1908 printing the illustrations are on the same paper as the text and are less clearly printed.

  d. A new edition, Constable & Co., n.d. with three additional coloured plates by John Campbell. Bound in red cloth gilt with a pictorial onlay.

10. **A Soul on Fire** by Florence Marryat. Sands & Co., London, 1898.
202 × 128 mm. 275 pp. + 14 pp. publisher's catalogue.
Cream cloth blocked in red and black with a design by WHR.
Reprinted 1902.
Note: The binding design is unsigned. Some copies of the book have a publisher's catalogue bound in that refers to this title as having a binding design by W. H. Robinson. Others have earlier catalogues bound in that do not refer to this title.

11. 'A Lullaby'.
Pall Mall Magazine, May 1898. Vol 15, p. 71.
A full page half-tone picture.

12. 'Peter the Cat' by Christopher Hare.
The Quiver, Jun 1898. pp. 753-758.
One half page and two smaller line drawings.

13. 'The Birth of the Crocus. A Fairy Parable' by Roma White.
The Quiver, Aug 1898. pp. 942-946.
One half page and two smaller line drawings.

1899

14a. **The Arabian Nights Entertainments**. Anon. George Newnes by arrangement with A. Constable & Co., London, 1899.
266 × 203 mm. 472 pp.
Pale green cloth with a pictorial design by WHR on front and spine printed in black, white, orange and brown. Bevel edged boards, black endpapers. Titled in gilt on front and spine, all edges gilt.
Many hundreds of illustrations by WHR, Helen Stratton, A. D. McCormick, A. L. Davis and A. E. Norbury, of which WHR contributed 18 full page and 189 smaller line drawings.
The book was also issued bound in pale blue cloth with the same design.

  b. Also published by A. Constable & Co., in 20 weekly parts in wrappers with a pictorial design by WHR printed in three colours.
Note: The original drawing for the illustration on p. 351 is in the British Museum.

15. **Fairy Tales From Hans Christian Andersen** translated by Mrs. E. Lucas, J. M. Dent & Co., London, 1899.

198 × 145 mm. xiv, 539 pp.

Green cloth printed in colours and gilt with a design of poppies and cherubs by Charles Robinson. Top edge gilt, others uncut. Red silk marker.

Illustrated by Thomas, Charles and Will Robinson. Chromolithographed frontispiece and title page, nine full page and 18 smaller line drawings, and pictorial endpapers by Charles; 16 full page and 17 smaller line drawings by Tom; and 13 full page and 22 smaller line drawings by Will. There are also a number of tailpiece vignettes, some used more than once, by Charles and Tom.

Reprinted by J. M. Dent in 1899, 1901, 1903, 1905, 1907, 1910, 1911, 1915, 1919, 1926, 1930, 1934 and 1939.

Note: The later printings have a less attractive binding with the original design printed in orange, brown and green only. This looks very dull compared with the reds, blues and gold of the original.

16a. **The Talking Thrush.** Stories of Birds and Beasts. Collected by W. Crooke and retold by W. H. D. Rouse. J. M. Dent & Co., London, 1899.

197 × 140 mm. xvi, 218 pp.

Green cloth printed in red and black with pictorial designs by WHR on front, spine and back.

Eight full page and 21 text illustrations, 30 vignettes and 23 pictorial initials, all in line. Pictorial title page in red and black.

Reprinted 1902, 1922.

b. A new edition published by J. M. Dent & Co., London, 1938.

191 × 134 mm. xii, 218 pp.

Bound in blue cloth printed in light blue and black with the original design on front and spine only. Beige dustwrapper.

Illustrated as earlier editions.

New title page using the centre vignette from the original design, with no border and the text typeset, printed in black only. List of illustrations omitted from this edition.

1900

17a. **The Poems of Edgar Allen Poe.** With an introduction by H. Noel Williams. George Bell and Sons, London, 1900.

204 × 133 mm. xxxviii, 225 pp.

Pale green cloth blocked in two darker shades of green and gilt with a design of trees by WHR.

Titled in gilt on the front and spine. Top edge gilt, others uncut.

Decorated title page in red and black, 27 full page and 76 smaller line drawings. Decorated endpapers.

Reprinted 1901. The balance of this printing reissued in 1907 with a cancel title page bearing that date.

b. A limited edition of 75 copies printed on Japanese vellum. George Bell and Sons, London, 1900.

Bound in beige canvas, titled in red and black on the spine.

The binding design for the front board printed in red and dark green bound in following the front endpaper and that for the spine bound in before the final endpaper. Edges trimmed.

c. Reprinted 1909 by George Bell and issued in a different binding decorated with a design of vine leaves by R. A. Bell. This was originally used for the volume of Shelley's poems published in the same series in 1902.

d. A new edition published by George Bell & Sons, London, 1970.

215 × 137 mm. xxii, 225 pp.

Black linson, blocked in silver and pink foil on the spine. Pictorial dustwrapper in red and black.

Illustrations as for the first edition, with a modified title page printed in black only.

Note: In this edition the long introduction to Poe's poetry by H. Noel Williams has been replaced by a short anonymous introduction to Heath Robinson's illustrations.

18. **Tales for Toby** by Ascot R. Hope. J. M. Dent & Co., London, 1900.
190 × 127 mm. 207 pp.
Green cloth printed in red and dark green with a pictorial design.
Top edge gilt, others uncut.
Illustrated by WHR and S. Jacobs. W.H.R. contributed the frontis and title page in red and black, five full page and four half page line drawings. The tailpieces throughout the book are unsigned, but are probably by WHR.

19. 'A Spanish Love Song'. A poem by Edwin Arnold.
The Ladies' Realm, Mar 1900. Vol 7, pp. 596-597.
Two full page line drawings with the text inset.

1901

20. **Fairy Tales from Hans Christian Andersen** translated by Mrs. E. Lucas. J. M. Dent & Co., London, 1901 in the 'Temple Classics for Young People' series.
152 × 94 mm. viii, 312 pp.
Dark blue cloth with a roundel in blind on the front and titled in gilt on the spine. Top edge gilt, others uncut. Red silk marker.
Illustrated by Charles, Tom and William Robinson, with chromolithographed frontispiece and title page and two full page line drawings by Charles, four full page line drawings by Tom and five by William. Also issued in a blue limp leather binding.
Note: All of the illustrations are taken from the 1899 edition at serial 15, except for the last, which is by William and illustrates 'The Ugly Duckling'.

21. 'The Widow and the Grain of Rice, a Siamese Parable' by Myra Hamilton.
The Quiver, Mar 1901. pp. 553-555.
Headpiece and one threequarter page illustration in line.

22. 'The Fairies' Dentist' by Myra Hamilton.
The Quiver, Oct 1901. pp. 1219-1222.
Headpiece and one threequarter page illustration in line.

1902

23. **The Adventures of Don Quixote of La Mancha** by Miguel de Cervantes. J. M. Dent & Co., London, 1902.
195 × 142 mm. xxii, 532 pp.
Green cloth printed in yellow and black with pictorial designs on the front, spine and back. Top edge gilt, others uncut.
Frontispiece and title page in red and black, 36 full page illustrations in pen and seven in chalk. Decorated endpapers printed in brown on green.
Reprinted 1919, 1923, 1931, 1936.
Note: The colours used for the binding varied in the reprints. The 1936 printing was issued in a dustwrapper printed in red and black on silver with the binding designs.

24a. **The Adventures of Uncle Lubin** written and illustrated by W. Heath Robinson.
Grant Richards, London, 1902.
201 × 154 mm. xviii, 118 pp. +1 p. advertisements.
Blue-green cloth blocked in white, red and green with a pictorial design. Blue

endpapers with pictorial designs printed in brown, different front and back. Coloured frontispiece. Pictorial titlepage and 15 pictorial half titles printed in red and black. Three double page, 43 full page and 64 smaller line drawings, and 44 decorative initials, these last printed in red.

b. A new edition published by Chatto & Windus, London, 1925.
207 × 153 mm. xvi, 118 pp.
Yellow cloth with a pictorial design and titles blocked in red.
Illustrated as the first edition, but with part of the title page and the decorative initials printed in blue. A new dustwrapper design in full colour was produced for this edition.

c. Another edition from Chatto & Windus, London, 1934. This is printed on slightly thicker paper than 24b. and apart from the coloured frontispiece, is printed in black only. The binding is yellow linson blocked in red as 24b.

d. A new edition published by The Minerva Press, London, 1972.
205 × 153 mm. xvi, 118 pp.
Yellow linson titled in blue on the spine. Top edge stained blue. Deep yellow dustwrapper with an illustration from the book in brown and titles in grey.
Printed in black and white throughout, including the frontispiece.
Reprinted subsequently on thinner paper. This printing was issued in either brown or yellow linson with a green dustwrapper printed in navy.

e. A new edition published by Penguin Books, London, 1975, in the 'Young Puffin' series.
197 × 127 mm. xiv, 118 pp. + 3 pp. advertisements.
Pictorial card covers printed in pink, brown and black with pictorial designs from the book front and back.
Printed from the Minerva Press edition with the frontispiece omitted.
Reprinted 1975.

25a. **Dent's Andersen in German** edited by Walter Rippmann. J. M. Dent & Co., London, 1902.
182 × 126 mm. xi, 219 pp.
Cream cloth printed in brown with an 'art nouveau' design signed 'K'.
Six full page and six smaller line drawings by WHR and four full page and two smaller line drawings by Charles Robinson.

b. Also issued with no vocabulary at the back. J. M. Dent & Co., London, 1902.
178 × 126 mm. ix, 108 pp.
Green cloth titled in brown on the front and spine.
In this issue the frontispiece by WHR and the list of illustrations are omitted.
Note: All of the illustrations were drawn for Dent's 1899 edition of Andersen's Fairy Tales. However, in that book the story 'The Ugly Duckling' had no illustrations. In this book that story has a full page and two smaller drawings by WHR. The full page drawing first appeared in Dent's 'Temple Classics' edition of Andersen's Fairy Tales (1901). One of the smaller drawings was used to illustrate 'The Marsh King's Daughter' in the 1899 Andersen. The other small drawing is published here for the first time.

26. **The House Annual, 1902.** Compiled by W. A. Morgan. Gale & Polden, London, 1902.
245 × 180 mm. viii, 144 pp. + 24 pp. advertisements.
Red cloth with 'art nouveau' decorations printed in black.
Frontispiece and 16 full page illustrations in line of which six are by WHR.
Note: This was a charity publication sold in aid of 'The Referee' Children's

Dinner Fund run by the Stock Exchange. The first five drawings by WHR illustrate 'Kittums' by Marie Corelli, 'Rich and Poor' by Clifton Bingham, 'The Fortunes of Ponto Fiennes' by Maj. A. Griffiths, 'The Cub in Love' by Coulson Kernahan, and 'The Usurper' by Howel Scratton. The sixth illustration stands alone and is titled 'A Curbstone Promoter'.

27a. **Mediaeval Stories** by Professor H. Shück, translated from the Swedish by W. F. Harvey, M.A. Sands & Co., London, 1902.

200 × 137 mm. xxii, 321 pp.

Brown cloth printed in dark brown with a pictorial design of a knight in armour by WHR. Titled in gilt on the spine. Top edge stained brown, others uncut.

Ten full page drawings on coated paper, decorated half-title and title, 13 pictorial headpieces and five vignettes, all in line.

b. Also issued in a red cloth binding blocked with a design in gilt.

28. **The Surprising Travels and Adventures of Baron Munchausen** by R. E. Raspe. Grant Richards, London, 1902.

173 × 114 mm. xx, 256 pp.

Blue cloth blocked in gilt with an 'art nouveau' design on front and spine. Top edge stained blue.

Four full page coloured plates and a title-page vignette.

29a. **Tales from Shakespeare** by Charles and Mary Lamb. Sands & Co., London, n.d. (1902).

207 × 138 mm. 296 pp.

Red morocco grained cloth decorated with illustrations from the book in gilt on the front and spine. Titled in gilt on front and spine. Top edge gilt. Uniform with *Danish Fairy Tales and Legends* (1897).

16 full page drawings on coated paper.

b. A new edition published by Alexander Gardner, Paisley, 1909.

202 × 144 mm. 296 pp.

Bound as the first edition.

Coloured frontispiece and 15 line drawings on coated paper.

Note: In the 1909 edition the plate illustrating 'A Midsummer Night's Dream' has replaced that for 'Macbeth' as the frontispiece and has been coloured. Unlike the Gardner reprint of *Danish Fairy Tales and Legends* with which it is uniform, this book has a revised list of illustrations reflecting the changes.

1903

30. **The Child's Arabian Nights** written and illustrated by W. Heath Robinson. Grant Richards, London, 1903.

245 × 188 mm. 84 pp.

Cloth backed pictorial boards with a design in full colour by WHR of an old man's head surrounded by children's heads.

12 full page plates chromolithographed by T. N. Storer & Sons and 25 smaller line drawings.

31. **Rama and the Monkeys** adapted for children from the Ramayana by Geraldine Hodgson. J. M. Dent & Co., London, 1903.

153 × 96 mm. xiii, 104 pp.

Blue morocco grained cloth with a roundel in blind on the front and titled in gilt on the spine. Top edge gilt, others uncut. Red silk marker.

Chromolithographed frontispiece and title page and six full page line drawings. There was an alternative limp leather binding.

32. **Boys' and Girls' Fairy Stories.** J. M. Dent & Co., London, 1903.
    180 × 119 mm. 156 pp. + 4 pp. advertisements.
    Stone coloured cloth printed in dark green and white with pictorial designs on the front and spine.
    16 coloured plates, six full page and 37 smaller illustrations of which three coloured plates and three full page line drawings are by WHR.
    Note: None of the illustrations in this book are attributed to artists or signed. However the illustrations to the stories 'Anna and the Fairies' and 'The Story of the Fisherman's Wife' are undoubtedly by Heath Robinson. Many of the other illustrations are by R. Anning Bell.

33. **Grant Richards's Children's Annual for 1904** edited by T. W. H. Crosland. Grant Richards, London, n.d. (1903)
    272 × 210. 200 pp.
    Bound in patterned linen with a design in green, blue, yellow and brown. Pictorial paper title label pasted on upper front board.
    33 full page coloured plates, five full page and 24 smaller line drawings of which two pairs of coloured plates and the title page vignette are by WHR.
    Note: The coloured plates were printed by Edmund Evans.

1904

34. **The Merry Multifleet and the Mounting Multicorps.** Created by Richard Johnson and put into writing by Thomas O'Cluny. J. M. Dent & Co., London, 1904.
    181 × 123 mm. xii, 206 pp.
    White cloth printed in red and black with a pictorial design by WHR on the front and spine.
    Three full page and 13 smaller line drawings.
    Reprinted 1907.

35a. **The Works of Mr. Francis Rabelais, Doctor in Physic Containing Five Books of the Lives, Heroick Deeds & Sayings of Gargantua and His Sonne Pantagruel.** Grant Richards, London, 1904. Two Volumes.
    285 × 222 mm. Vol I, xlii, 377 pp. Vol II, xliv, 350 pp.
    White coarse weave cloth blocked in gilt on the front and spine with an 'art nouveau' design of a vine climbing a tree. Top edge gilt, others uncut. Pictorial endpapers different front and back.
    Vol I has a photogravure frontispiece, 55 full page illustrations, 59 grotesque heads and 26 other small drawings or vignettes, all in line.
    Vol II has a photogravure frontispiece, 43 full page illustrations, 35 grotesque heads and 34 other small drawings or vignettes, all in line.

  b. An edition-de-luxe limited to 25 copies numbered and signed by the artist was also issued. The advertisement for this states that 'five of the photogravure illustrations are in duplicate also signed by the artist'. This is an imprecise statement since only the two frontispieces are printed from photogravure blocks. Presumably these were in duplicate together with three other full page illustrations.

  c. A new edition published by Alexander Moring Ltd., London, n.d. (1913) in two volumes.
    220 × 142 mm. Vol I, xvi, 474 pp. Vol II, xvi, 462 pp.
    Dark blue cloth titled in gilt on the front and spine, top edge gilt.
    Vol I has a half-tone frontispiece printed in black, 55 full page illustrations and 73 vignettes and grotesque heads.
    Vol II has a half-tone frontispiece printed in sepia, 43 full page illustrations and 65 vignettes and grotesque heads.

d. A new edition published by The Navarre Society, London, 1921, in two volumes. 228 × 146mm. Vol I, xvi, 474pp. Vol II, xvi, 462pp.
White cloth blocked on the spine with the original design and on the front with a fleur-de-lys. Grey dustwrappers printed in navy. Top edges gilt, others uncut.
Illustrated as the 1913 edition.
Reprinted n.d. in two volumes.

e. Reprinted by The Navarre Society, London, 1931. Two volumes bound as one, page size reduced to 213 × 136mm.
Red cloth blocked in gilt on the spine and blind on the front.
Illustrated as the 1913 edition, but without the frontispieces.

f. Reprinted by The Navarre Society, London, 1948. Two volumes bound as one.
Bound in blue cloth blocked gilt on the spine with a new design. Illustrated as the 1931 printing.

g. Reprinted by The Navarre Society, London, 1954.
As f, but bound in red cloth gilt.

36. **Grant Richards's Children's Annual for 1905** edited by T. W. H. Crosland and W. Collinge. Grant Richards, London, n.d. (1904)
272 × 210mm. 200pp.
Bound in patterned linen with a design in green, blue, yellow and pink. Pictorial paper title label pasted on front board.
33 full page coloured plates and 39 line drawings of which one pair of coloured plates and the title page vignette are by WHR.

37. 'Sanota. A Red Indian Story', by Catherine Bearne.
Sunday Reading for the Young, 1904. Pages 68-70, 74-75, 86-88, 98-100, 119-120, 123, 130-132, 142-144, 147, 156-158.
Seven full page line drawings.

1905

38. **Kingdoms Curious** by Myra Hamilton. Wm. Heinemann Ltd., London, 1905.
210 × 147mm. xi, 248pp.
Buff cloth blocked in black and gilt with a pictorial design based on a drawing by Mary Miles.
19 full page and 14 smaller line drawings by various artists of which one full page and one smaller drawing are by WHR.
Note: These stories were collected from *Cassell's Magazine, The Quiver, Little Folks* and *The Bystander*. The two illustrations by WHR are to 'The Fairies' Dentist' which first appeared in *The Quiver*, Oct 1901. Other illustrators include A. Rackham and H. R. Millar.

39a. **Stories from Chaucer** Told to the Children by Janet Harvey Kelman. T. C. & E. C. Jack, London, n.d. (1905).
143 × 110mm. xi, 114pp.
Issued in two bindings:
  i. Green cloth decorated in gilt with a coloured pictorial onlay. Top edge gilt, others uncut.
  ii. Grey or brown paper covered boards decorated in black with a pictorial onlay. Edges uncut.
Eight full page coloured plates, one of which was repeated as the onlay.
Note: The publisher's catalogue lists this as number three in the 'Told to the Children' series. It was also issued with volumes of stories from Shakespeare and Spenser as a set of three books in a gilt decorated cloth case.

b. A new edition from T. C. & E. C. Jack, London, n.d. (Ca. 1930)
144 × 114mm. xi, 114pp.

Red cloth with a pictorial design printed in black.
Eight full page coloured plates.

c. A new edition published by Thomas Nelson & Sons Ltd., London, n.d. (1951)
156 × 103 mm. viii, 114 pp.
Red linson titled in black. Yellow pictorial dustwrapper.
Eight full page coloured plates.

40. **The Children's Christmas Treasury of Things New and Old.** J. M. Dent & Co., London, n.d. (1905)
264 × 200 mm. 208 pp.
White cloth printed in many colours with a pictorial design by Reginald Knowles. Top edge gilt, others uncut.
32 coloured plates and 26 line drawings by various artists of which three full page drawings in full colour, three full page and one half page drawing in red and black and a headpiece and tailpiece in line are by WHR.
Note: Of the Heath Robinson drawings two full page humorous coloured drawings had not been previously published. Nor had the illustrations to 'The Monkey's Revenge' by E. V. Lucas, comprising one full page and one half page line drawing in red and black and a tailpiece in line. The other drawings had appeared in previous Dent publications, colour having been added for this edition.

41. 'Septimus Septimusson. A Fairy Story' by E. Nesbit.
Pall Mall Magazine, Dec 1905. Vol 36, pp. 711-719.
One full page, three half page illustrations and a tailpiece, all in half-tone with borders in line.

1906

42. **The Memoirs of Barry Lyndon** and **Men's Wives** by W. M. Thackeray. The Caxton Publishing Company, London, n.d. (1906).
203 × 127 mm. xii, 358 pp.
Blue cloth decorated in white and titled in gilt on the spine.
Sepia gravure frontispiece by Gordon Browne. Three full page coloured plates and three sepia line drawings by WHR.

43a. **Stories from the Iliad or the Seige of Troy** Told to the Children by Jeanie Lang. T. C. & E. C. Jack, London, n.d. (1906)
147 × 113 mm. vii, 119 pp.
Issued in two bindings:
i. Brown cloth decorated in gilt with a pictorial onlay. Top edge gilt, others uncut.
ii. Brown paper covered boards decorated in black with a pictorial onlay. Edges uncut.
Eight full page coloured plates of which one was repeated as the onlay.
Note: The illustrations are reduced from original watercolours measuring 240 × 180 mm, i.e. twice the height of the printed plates. This book was number 22 in the 'Told to the Children' series.

b. A new edition from T. C. & E. C. Jack, London, n.d.
144 × 114 mm. vii, 119 pp.
Red cloth with a pictorial design printed in black.
Eight full page coloured plates.

c. A new edition published by Thomas Nelson & Sons Ltd., London, n.d.
156 × 103 mm. v, 119 pp.
Green linson titled in black. Yellow pictorial dustwrapper.
Eight full page coloured plates.

44a. **Stories from the Odyssey** Told to the Children by Jeanie Lang. T. C. & E. C. Jack, London, n.d. (1906)

147 × 113 mm. ix, 118 pp.

Issued in two bindings:

i. Brown cloth decorated in gilt with a pictorial onlay. Top edge gilt, others uncut.

ii. Brown paper covered boards decorated in black with a pictorial onlay. Edges uncut.

Eight full page coloured plates of which one was repeated as the onlay.

Note: On the verso of the original watercolour for the last plate are notes on reproduction dated 22.12.05. This book was number 25 in the 'Told to the Children' series.

b. A new edition from T. C. & E. C. Jack, London, n.d.

144 × 114 mm. ix, 118 pp.

Blue cloth with a pictorial design printed in black.

Eight full page coloured plates.

c. A new edition published by Thomas Nelson & Sons Ltd., London, n.d.

156 × 103 mm. vii, 118 pp.

Blue linson titled in black. Yellow pictorial dustwrapper.

Eight full page coloured plates.

45. **Fairy Tales from Hans Christian Andersen**. J. M. Dent & Co., London, 1906. In the Everyman series.

173 × 106 mm. x, 387 pp.

Blue cloth decorated in gilt on the spine. Top edge stained blue.

Illustrations by Charles, Tom and William Robinson taken from Dent's 1899 edition.

One full page and two smaller drawings by Charles, two full page and three smaller drawings by Tom and one full page and ten smaller drawings by William. The tailpieces are by Charles and Tom, and the title page decorations, although unsigned, are almost certainly by Charles.

The first printing was in Feb 1906 and the second in April.

It was reprinted in 1907, 1909, 1911, 1914, 1916, 1918, 1922 et. seq. finally disappearing from Dent's list in 1960.

There are variations in binding over the years including some issues in limp leather.

46. 'What Creature Would You Prefer to Be?' A symposium of reader's answers.
Pearson's Magazine, Apr 1906. Vol 21, pp. 431-440.
Nine line drawings of various sizes.

47. 'The Story of a Successful Author'. A humorous poem by Alice J. Petherick.
Pearson's Magazine, Jun 1906. Vol 21, pp. 676-677.
Five small line drawings.

48. 'The Pro. A Curious Cricket Story' by P. G. Wodehouse.
Pearson's Magazine, Aug. 1906. Vol 22, pp. 170-177.
One half page and three smaller half-tone illustrations.

49. 'The Peach Stone' by W. H. Bryce-Stacpoole.
Pall Mall Magazine, Dec 1906. Vol 38, pp. 789-796.
One full page, two half page and two vignette half-tone illustrations.

50. 'The Little Folks Home' conducted by Bella Sidney Woolf.
Little Folks, Dec 1906. Vol 65, pp. 116-122.
One half page illustration in line and yellow.
This special Christmas number also has two other full page drawings in line and colour by WHR, 'The Friendly Elf' at p. 45 and 'At the Seaside' at p. 126.
Note: This special number, first issued in Dec 1906, was subsequently incorporated in the half-yearly volume for Jan-Jun 1907.

1907

51a. **The Monarchs of Merry England (William I to Richard III)** by Roland Carse. Alf
    Cooke, Leeds and London, n.d. (1907)
    284 × 220 mm. Pages unnumbered (126 pp)
    and its sequel:
    More Monarchs of Merry England (Henry VII to Edward VII) by Roland Carse.
    T. Fisher Unwin, London, n.d. (1908)
    280 × 216 mm. Pages unnumbered (130 pp).
    Each volume is bound in quarter red cloth, grey-blue boards printed in three
    colours with pictorial designs front and back.
    Pictorial endpapers.
    Each volume has 20 full page coloured plates and 73 small line drawings or
    vignettes.
    Note: The British Library copy of this work is bound in four parts, with ten
    coloured plates to each part, in cloth backed boards with a duplicate colour
    plate mounted on the front of each part and the title printed on the front in black
    and white. This is probably a pre-publication binding that never reached the
    shops.

  b. A new reduced edition published in four parts subtitled 'William I to Henry III',
    'Edward I to Richard III', 'Henry VII to Elizabeth' and 'James I to Edward VII'
    respectively. Alf Cooke, Leeds, n.d.
    275 × 209 mm.
    Card covers printed with one of the coloured illustrations from the original
    volumes.
    Two other coloured plates and the original line drawings and vignettes in each
    part.

52. **The Secret Woman** by Eden Phillpotts.
    Collins Clear Type Press, London, n.d. (1907)
    155 × 100 mm. 384 pp.
    Blue cloth decorated in gilt on the spine.
    Coloured frontispiece and pictorial title page.
    Note: Published in 'Collins Modern Fiction' series.

53. 'Gwendoline's Burglar'. A Simple Narrative by Frank Savile.
    Pearson's Magazine, Jun 1907. Vol 23, pp. 647-651.
    Pictorial headpiece and three small line drawings.

54. 'Wonderkin' by A. E. Bonser.
    Little Folks, Jul 1907. Vol 66, pp. 91-94.
    One half page line drawing.

55. 'Mernippers at Play' and 'The Intelligent Hobgoblin'.
    Little Folks, Dec 1907. Vol 67, pp. 19 and 61.
    Two full page line drawings, one in blue and black and the other in red and black.

1908

56. **The Book of Witches** by O. M. Hueffer. Eveleigh Nash, London, 1908.
    223 × 138 mm. xi, 336 pp.
    Bound in cloth, top edge gilt.
    Coloured frontispiece.

57a. **Twelfth Night or What You Will** by William Shakespeare. Hodder & Stoughton,
    London, n.d. (1908).
    247 × 185 mm. xxiv, 144 pp.
    Green cloth blocked in gilt with pictorial designs and titles on front and spine.

Top edge stained green, green dustwrapper titled in dark green with pictorial onlay. Dark green endpapers.

40 coloured plates tipped onto dark green mounts. Pictorial title-page, five half titles, and tailpiece vignette in line.

Reissued (n.d.) with plates on white mounts with ochre borders, white endpapers.

b. A signed limited edition of 350 copies printed on handmade paper and bound in white vellum, gilt.

c. Reprinted, n.d. (ca. 1916) with newly drawn pictorial endpaper designs printed in grey and green on cream paper. Cream card mounts with decorative borders in grey and gold, otherwise as the first edition.

d. A new edition. Hodder & Stoughton, London, n.d. (ca. 1920).
245 × 180 mm. xxiv, 144 pp.
Lilac cloth printed with designs in brown and titled in green on the front and gilt on the spine. Plain endpapers.
24 coloured plates tipped on to cream card mounts with decorative borders in grey and gold. Line decorations as first edition.

e. A new edition. Hodder & Stoughton, New York and London, n.d.
248 × 181 mm. 144 pp.
Green cloth blocked in black with a pictorial design (not by WHR).
Titled in gilt on front and spine.
16 coloured plates tipped onto pages with printed borders of dots. Line decorations as first edition.

58a. **The Arabian Nights**. A. Constable & Co. Ltd., London, n.d. (1908).
192 × 136 mm. xvi, 435 pp.
Grey cloth printed in full colour with a pictorial design. Top edge stained grey.
Coloured frontispiece and title page by Helen Stratton. 36 full page and 44 smaller line drawings by WHR and 20 full page and 24 smaller line drawings by Helen Stratton.

b. Reprinted for G. Selfridge & Co., 1911.

c. Reprinted by Constable & Co., n.d. bound in light blue cloth printed with a pictorial design in black on the front and gilt on the spine, poorly printed.
Note: All of the illustrations except the frontispiece are taken from the 1899 edition.

59. 'The Shovewood. A Naval Episode' by C. C. A. Stuart, R.N.
Pearson's Magazine, May 1908. Vol 25, pp. 553-557.
Headpiece and two small illustrations in half tone.

60. 'Why I am Not a Criminal'. Anon.
Strand Magazine, Jun 1908. Vol 35, pp. 662-667.
Six threequarter page, half-tone illustrations.

1909

61a. **A Song of the English** by Rudyard Kipling. Hodder & Stoughton, London, n.d. (1909).
280 × 218 mm. Pages unnumbered (128 pp. excluding mounts).
Dark blue cloth blocked in gilt with pictorial designs on the front and spine. Issued in a decorated box.
Pictorial title page in red and black. 30 coloured plates tipped onto cream card mounts with coloured decorative borders. Titled tissue guards each with a miniature line illustration. 59 line illustrations, half page or smaller.

b. A signed, limited edition of 500 copies printed on handmade paper and bound in vellum with a cover design in red, green and gold.

c. A reduced edition, Hodder & Stoughton, London, n.d. (1912).
199 × 145 mm. Pages unnumbered.
Dark blue cloth blocked in gilt on the front with a design of St. George and the dragon, taken from the original title page. Issued in a blue box with white labels printed in gold and a mounted plate on the top. Pictorial endpapers printed in pale blue. Top edge gilt. 12 coloured plates, and line drawings as the first edition.
Printed on the right hand pages only.

d. A cheap edition, Hodder & Stoughton, London, n.d. (1912).
199 × 145 mm. Pages unnumbered.
Blue cloth printed in black.
Eight monochrome plates and line drawings as the first edition.
Printed on the right hand pages only.

e. A new edition, Hodder & Stoughton, for *The Daily Telegraph*, London, n.d. (1915)
275 × 213 mm. 91 pp.
Cream cloth blocked in dark blue. Cream dustwrapper.
16 coloured plates tipped onto brown card mounts under captioned tissue guards.
Note: This edition was sold in aid of *The Daily Telegraph* National Bands Fund. It was issued with a 4 pp. speech by Rudyard Kipling given at the Mansion House on 27th January, 1915 loosely inserted.

f. A new edition, Hodder & Stoughton, London, n.d. (1919).
246 × 182 mm. 123 pp.
Dark blue cloth printed with a design in light blue and titled in gilt on the front and spine. Cream dustwrapper printed in blue with a mounted colour plate.
16 coloured plates tipped onto cream mounts and line drawings as the first edition.
Note: This edition was still in print in 1925.

62. 'Mr. Broadbent's Information' by Henry A. Hering.
Pearson's Magazine, Mar 1909. Vol 27, pp. 266-274.
A headpiece and two full page illustrations in half tone.

1910

63. **The Collected Verse of Rudyard Kipling**. Doubleday, Page & Co., New York, 1910.
248 × 178 mm. 392 pp.
Red cloth blocked in gilt with elaborate designs on front and spine. Top edge gilt.
Nine coloured plates on Japanese vellum mounts with decorated borders and captioned tissue guards. Decorated title page and five pictorial section titles in red and black, eight full page line drawings and a pictorial headpiece.
Note: This book was not published in England.

64. **The Dead King**. A poem by Rudyard Kipling. Hodder & Stoughton, London, 1910.
204 × 144 mm. Pages unnumbered (48 pp.).
Purple cloth blocked in gilt on the front with the title and the head of Edward VII.
Pictorial title page in purple and black, decorated half title, 13 pictorial or decorative borders to the verses and eight vignettes.
Printed on the right hand page of each opening only.
Also issued in purple paper wrappers embossed with the head of Edward VII in silver.

65. 'A Modern Version of Cinderella' by Helen Sheringham.
Royal Magazine, Aug 1910. Vol 24, pp. 375-378.
One full page and two smaller half tone illustrations.

1911

66. **The Golden Treasury of Songs and Lyrics** compiled by F. T. Palgrave. Hodder & Stoughton, London, n.d. (1911).

194 × 145 mm. xvi, 459 pp.

Plum cloth decorated in gilt and black on front and spine.

18 coloured plates, tipped onto beige mounts, by various artists, including one by WHR taken from Twelfth Night.

Note: The WHR plate illustrates the line 'Come Away, Come Away, Death'.

67. **The Odd Volume** edited by John G. Wilson. Simkin, Marshall, Hamilton, Kent & Co. Ltd., London, 1911.

250 × 186 mm. 96 pp. + lx pp. advertisements.

Grey paper wrappers printed in navy blue, pictorial onlay.

13 coloured plates and 26 full page black and white illustrations by various artists of which one coloured plate and one pencil drawing are by WHR.

Note: This compilation was published in aid of the funds of the National Book Trade Provident Society.

68. Decorative headpieces for *The Sketch*.

A set of 18 different headpieces in line for regular articles in *The Sketch*. They first appeared on 26th April 1911 and remained in use until 1917 when they were gradually replaced by a new set drawn by Gladys Peto.

1912

69a. **Bill the Minder** written and illustrated by W. Heath Robinson. Constable & Co. Ltd., London, 1912.

242 × 184 mm. xvi, 256 pp.

Green cloth decorated in gilt on front and spine, with a trimmed version of the coloured frontispiece mounted on the front board. 16 coloured plates mounted on Japanese vellum. Pictorial title page, 25 full page and 100 smaller line drawings.

b. A signed limited edition of 380 copies printed on hand-made paper and bound in vellum decorated in gilt with a design taken from p. 1 of the book. Yellow silk ties.

c. An issue of the 1912 printing with only eight coloured plates, bound in red cloth decorated in gilt with a small ivory and gilt onlay on the upper front board.

d. Another issue of the 1912 printing with only four coloured plates, bound in blue cloth printed in black and titled in gilt.

e. Reissued with a cancel title page by Constable & Co. Ltd., London, 1915, with 16 coloured plates.

230 × 180 mm. xvi, 256 pp.

Blue cloth printed in black and titled in gilt, with a miniature coloured plate mounted on the upper front board.

f. An issue with the 1915 title page with only 12 coloured plates, bound in blue cloth printed in black with a small ivory and gilt onlay as 69c.

g. An issue with the 1915 title page with only nine coloured plates, bound as 69f.

h. A new edition published by Hodder & Stoughton, London, n.d. (1924).

233 × 158 mm.

Yellow cloth printed in red and black with a pictorial design crudely adapted from page one of the book.

16 tipped in coloured plates and line drawings as first edition.

i. Reprinted by Hodder & Stoughton, n.d. (ca. 1930) bound in royal blue cloth decorated in blind and titled in gilt on the spine.

j. A new edition, Hodder & Stoughton, London, 1982.

240 × 175 mm. 254 pp.

Blue cloth blocked in gilt on the front and spine as for the limited edition.
Illustrated as the first edition but with the coloured plates on glossy paper with grey surrounds to simulate mounts.

k. A limited issue of 250 copies of the 1982 edition bound in full morocco grained blue leather blocked in gilt, all edges gilt. Blue slipcase.

70. **Happy Hearts**. A Picture Book for Boys and Girls edited by Harry Golding. Ward, Lock & Co. Ltd., London, 1912.
275 × 216 mm. 182 pp.
Quarter blue cloth, pictorial front board with a coloured picture by WHR showing an old lady and nine children tobogganing.
Illustrated with 11 coloured plates and numerous line drawings by various artists, of which two chromolithographed plates are by WHR.
Note: The WHR plates illustrate 'The Stowaways' by Agnes Crozier Herbertson and 'Good Sport' by E.S. Other Illustrators include John Hassall, G.E. Studdy and Louis Wain.

71. 'The Three Princesses of Connaught' by Seumas MacManus.
Royal Magazine, Jan 1912. Vol 27, pp. 221-227.
One full page and two smaller half-tone illustrations.

72. 'A School for Poets' by C.E.B. of *The Evening News* (Claude Burton).
London Magazine, Jul 1912. Vol 28, pp. 595-600.
One threequarter page, two half page and one small half-tone illustrations.

73. 'The Pluperfect House' by Keble Howard.
Windsor Magazine, Dec 1912. Vol 37, pp. 157-163.
Two half page half-tone illustrations.

1913

74a. **Hans Andersen's Fairy Tales**. Constable & Co. Ltd., London, 1913.
246 × 185 mm. xii, 289 pp.
Red cloth decorated in gilt on the front and spine, with a white and gilt onlay on the front. Top edge stained red.
16 coloured plates tipped onto cream mounts with ochre borders under captioned tissue guards. Pictorial title page, 37 full page and 58 smaller illustrations in line.

b. A signed limited edition of 100 copies printed on handmade paper and bound in full vellum decorated in gilt.

c. Reissued with a cancel title page dated 1917 on the verso. Bound in red cloth printed with the original designs in dark red. Top edge stained red.

d. A new edition published by Hodder & Stoughton, London, n.d. (1923).
233 × 157 mm. 320 pp.
Yellow cloth blocked in blue and black with a pictorial design from 'The Nightingale' on the front. Top edge stained brown.
Illustrations as for the first edition, but less clearly printed.
Endpapers decorated with illustrations from the book in blue.

e. A reprint of the 1923 edition, Hodder & Stoughton, n.d., bound in red cloth blocked in gilt on the front with the pictorial design from p. 11 and titled in gilt on the spine. Top edge gilt.

f. A new edition published by Hodder & Stoughton for Boots Pure Drug Co. Ltd., n.d. (1927).
250 × 188 mm. 320 pp.
Bound in red cloth printed in black and blocked in gilt with the pictorial design from the top of the contents page. Titled in gilt on the front and spine.

Illustrations as the 1923 edition.

g. Another reprint of the 1923 edition, Hodder & Stoughton, n.d., bound in blue cloth decorated in blind and titled in gilt. Blue dustwrapper with a pictorial onlay.

h. A new edition in two volumes published by Pan Books Ltd., London, 1976 in the Piccolo Gift Books Series.
   222 × 177 mm. 144 pp. and 152 pp.
   Pictorial card wrappers.
   Illustrated as earlier editions, but with the coloured plates in pairs printed back to back.

i. A new edition published by Hodder & Stoughton, London, 1981.
   240 × 175 mm. 288 pp.
   Brown cloth blocked in gilt with the designs used for the first edition, but without the white panel.
   Illustrated as the first edition, but with the coloured plates printed on glossy paper with cream surrounds to simulate mounts.

j. A limited issue of 500 copies of the 1981 edition bound in full brown leather and issued in a slipcase.

75. **The Countryside**. First piano lessons. Book II. Composed by Walter Carroll. Forsyth Brothers Limited, London, n.d. (1913).
   311 × 244 mm. 16 pp.
   Front cover illustration in line printed in green.
   Note: This was probably reprinted many times. Later printings have notice of renewed copyright at the foot of the first page of music.

76. 'Exiled by Order of Nijinsky: The Spirit of the Old Regime'.
   The Sketch, 23 Jul 1913. p. I of supplement.
   A full page drawing in pen and pencil.
   Note: This drawing, which is the frontispiece to a supplement on 'The Dance', is in the style of the drawings for *A Midsummer Night's Dream* and completely unlike Heath Robinson's regular work for this magazine.

1914

77. **Shakespeare's Comedy of a Midsummer Night's Dream**. Constable & Co. Ltd., London, 1914.
   286 × 222 mm. xvi, 188 pp.
   Grey cloth blocked in gilt, mauve, ochre, pink and two shades of blue with a pictorial design. Edges uncut.
   12 coloured plates tipped onto cream mounts with beige ruled borders. 46 full page and 17 smaller line drawings.

b. A signed limited edition of 250 copies printed on handmade paper of which only 100 were issued in 1914 bound in vellum gilt with a white silk marker.

c. A second issue of the first edition bound in blue cloth printed in black with the original design.

d. A third issue of the first edition (in 1919) bound in quarter beige cloth with green boards, titled in black on the spine. Brown dustwrapper printed with the original binding design in black.

e. The balance of the signed, limited edition issued (in 1919) in quarter green cloth, green boards, paper label on spine.

f. A new edition published by The Minerva Press, London, 1976.
   244 × 175 mm. x, 150 pp.

Green linson titled in gilt on the spine. Top edge stained brown. Cream pictorial dustwrapper printed in green and brown.

This edition has none of the coloured plates, but reproduces all but two of the line drawings. These are reproduced at the same size as the earlier printing, but with smaller margins.

78. **Tales from Shakespeare** by Charles and Mary Lamb. Hodder & Stoughton, London, n.d. (1914).

192 × 146 mm. x, 380 pp.

Blue buckram blocked in black and gilt (uniform with *The Golden Treasury*, 1911). 16 coloured plates tipped onto beige mounts. Various artists. Two of the plates are by WHR, taken from *Twelfth Night*.

Note: The WHR plates are those which in *Twelfth Night* illustrate the lines 'O, when mine eyes did see Olivia first' and 'O time! thou must untangle this, not I.'

79. 'The Death of Rancing Roarer' by Norah M. Craggs.

Strand Magazine, Dec 1914. Vol 48, pp. 786-793.

Four illustrations in line of which one is full page, one is threequarter page and two extend across two pages each.

1915

80a. **The Water-Babies. A Fairy Tale for a Land-Baby** by Charles Kingsley. Constable & Co. Ltd., London, 1915.

215 × 166 mm. x, 320 pp.

Green cloth blocked in gilt with a pictorial design on the front and spine. Top edge stained green. Cream dustwrapper printed in red and black.

Eight coloured plates, 52 full page and 52 smaller line drawings.

Also issued in a cheaper green binding printed in black and in full leather.

b. A facsimile reprint published by Constable & Co. Ltd., London, 1975. This edition, printed by offset lithography, is bound in pale green linson printed in black and has a full colour pictorial dustwrapper.

Reprinted 1979.

81. 'How the Sea Became Salt' A Norwegian story for children retold in English by E. Dyke.

Strand Magazine, Apr 1915. Vol 49, pp. 467-471.

Three illustrations in line of which one extends across two pages and two extend diagonally across one page each.

82. 'The Sea Goblins'. From the Swedish.

Strand Magazine, Jun 1915. Vol 49, pp. 713-719.

Four illustrations in line of which two extend across two pages and two are half page.

83. 'The Idle Fellow'. A Russian Fairy Tale.

Strand Magazine, Jul 1915. Vol 50, pp. 114-119.

Three illustrations in line of which two extend across two pages and one fills most of another page.

84. 'Jack, or the Golden Snuff Box'. A fairy story for children.

Strand Magazine, Aug 1915. Vol 50, pp. 228-233.

Three illustrations in line of which two extend across two pages and one is half page.

85. 'Stupider and Stupider'. A story for children from the Slavonic.

Strand Magazine, Oct 1915. Vol 50, pp. 476-479.

Two line drawings each extending across two pages.

86. 'The Ogres of Ojejama'. A story for children from the Japanese.
    Strand Magazine, Nov 1915. Vol 50, pp. 596-599.
    Two line drawings each extending across two pages.

87. 'The Competition at the Castlebar' by Morley Roberts.
    Strand Magazine, Dec 1915. Vol 50, pp. 603-612.
    Four half-tone illustrations of which one fills one and a half pages, two fill three-quarters of a page and one is half page.

88. 'Biddulph. A Tale of a Magic Pool' written and illustrated by W. Heath Robinson.
    Pearson's Magazine, Dec 1915. Vol 40, pp. 726-731.
    One double page, one full page and three smaller line drawings.

1916

89. **Peacock Pie**. A book of rhymes by Walter de la Mare. Constable & Co. Ltd., London, n.d. (1916).
    215 × 167mm. viii, 180pp.
    Dark green cloth decorated with an ivory and gilt pictorial panel, 75 × 80mm., on the front and titled in gilt on the front and spine. Green dustwrapper printed in dark blue.
    Coloured frontispiece, pictorial title page, 25 full page line drawings, eight pictorial section titles and 61 smaller drawings. Pictorial endpapers printed in brown on cream.
    Reprinted 1920 with plain endpapers.

90. **The Queen's Gift Book**. Hodder & Stoughton, London, n.d. (1916)
    245 × 183mm. 160pp.
    Light blue cloth blocked in dark blue.
    Many illustrations in colour and black and white by various artists. WHR contributed one coloured plate, which is tipped onto a grey card mount, and three line drawings to illustrate 'The Man of Words' by Mrs. Henry de la Pasture.

91. **Princess Marie-Jose's Children's Book**. Cassell & Company, London, n.d. (1916).
    233 × 167mm. 128pp.
    Cloth backed pictorial boards.
    Many illustrations in colour and black and white by various artists of which one coloured plate is by WHR.
    Note: The WHR picture was first published as a line drawing on p. 32 of *Bill the Minder* and was coloured for this compilation.

92. **The Book of Limericks** by Sir William Bull and 'Orion' of the *Daily Express* (William Warren).
    Daily Express, London, 1916.
    182 × 244mm. 96pp.
    Quarter red cloth, flush cut beige boards printed in red and black.
    109 line drawings including one very rough sketch by WHR.
    Reprinted same year.

93. **Forest Fantasies**. Nine miniatures for pianoforte composed by Walter Carroll.
    Forsyth Brothers Ltd., London and Manchester, n.d. (1916).
    309 × 244mm. 16pp.
    Front cover and title page illustrations in line.
    Note: The first printing had the words 'war edition' at the head of the title page. The music was probably reprinted many times and later printings have notice of renewed copyright at the foot of the first page of music.

94. **Playbox Annual for 1917**. Amalgamated Press, London, n.d. (1916).
    Contains the following stories illustrated by WHR: 'The Idle Fellow', pp. 35-40,

three illustrations printed in red and black; 'How the Sea Became Salt', pp. 81-85, three illustrations printed in green.
Note: The stories and illustrations first appeared in *The Strand Magazine* in 1915.

95. 'The Hat Full of Soldiers'. A story for children from the Bohemian.
Strand Magazine, Jan 1916. Vol 51, pp. 103-107.
Two line drawings each extending across two pages.

96. 'The Astragen Waistcoat. How it Ameliorated Certain Grave Acerbities in the Courtship of Aloysius Moriarty' by E. A. Morphy.
Strand Magazine, Feb. 1916. Vol 51, pp. 130-139.
Three half-tone illustrations of which two cover one and a half pages each and the third threequarters of a page.

97. 'What the Snake Did for Jacolino'. A story for children by E. Dyke.
Strand Magazine, Feb 1916. Vol 51, pp. 219-223.
Three illustrations in line of which one is full page and two extend across two pages.

98. 'Prince Roshun'. A story for children by Rani Goss.
Strand Magazine, Mar 1916. Vol 51, pp. 328-332.
Three illustrations in line of which two extend across two pages and the other is half page.

99. 'The Knight of the Scissors and Thimble'. Anon.
Strand Magazine, Apr 1916. Vol 51, pp. 434-439.
Two line drawings each extending across two pages.

100. 'Two Goats, a Garden and —' by Elizabeth Allison.
Strand Magazine, Sep 1916. Vol 52, pp. 311-313.
Four small line drawings.

101. 'Nothing to What I Once Saw' from the French of Edouard Osmont.
Strand Magazine, Oct 1916. Vol 52, pp. 466-469.
One threequarter page line drawing and one extending across two pages.

102. 'The Rusty Pot and the Wooden Balls'. A story for children.
Strand Magazine, Nov 1916. Vol 52, pp. 573-577.
Two line drawings each extending across two pages.

103. 'The Three Faithful Companions'. A fairy legend retold by A. H. Greenwood.
Strand Magazine, Dec 1916. Vol 52, pp. 733-738.
Three line drawings of which two are half page and the third extends across two pages.
Note: Two of the illustrations have been slightly reduced to allow more room for the text. They were subsequently printed complete in *Playbox Annual for 1919*.

1917

104. **Playbox Annual for 1918**. Amalgamated Press, London, n.d. (1917)
Contains the following stories illustrated by WHR:
'The Magic Scissors and Thimble', pp. 65-71, three illustrations printed in green.
'Jacolino the Farmer's Boy', pp. 101-105, three illustrations printed in red and black.
'Prince Roshun', pp. 162-166, three illustrations printed in black.
Note: The stories and illustrations first appeared in *The Strand Magazine* in 1916, the first as 'The Knight of the Scissors and Thimble' and the second as 'What the Snake Did for Jacolino'. The third title is unchanged.

105. 'What the Zeppelin Dropped — Part I. How Conrad an Uncultured Indian Captured' edited by J. Storer Clouston.

Pearson's Magazine, Jan 1917. Vol 43, pp. 60-64.
One full page and one smaller half tone illustration.

106. 'What the Zeppelin Dropped — Part II. The Brave Aged Baron and Little Brave Frederick' edited by J. Storer Clouston.
Pearson's Magazine, Feb 1917. Vol 43, pp. 106-109.
One full page half-tone illustration.

107. 'What the Zeppelin Dropped — Part III. How England Must of Hans Beware' edited by J. Storer Clouston.
Pearson's Magazine, Mar 1917. Vol 43, pp. 232-235.
One full page half-tone illustration.

108. 'One Arabian Night'. A story for children by Elsie E. Dill.
Strand Magazine, Jul 1917. Vol 54, pp. 92-95.
Two line drawings of which one extends across two pages and the other diagonally across one page.

109. 'Kill or Cure' by Laurence Housman.
Strand Magazine, Dec 1917. Vol 54, pp. 633-641.
Six line drawings heightened with red and grey washes of which two extend across two pages, one extends diagonally across one page and the others fill one third of a page each.

110. 'The Camouflage Tree'. A poem by W.K.H.
Pearson's Magazine, Dec 1917. Vol 44, pp. 424-425.
Two full page half tone illustrations with the text inset.

1918

111. **Playbox Annual for 1919**. Amalgamated Press, London, n.d. (1918).
Contains the following stories illustrated by WHR:
'The Three Faithful Companions', pp. 37-44, three illustrations printed in blue.
'The Hat Full of Soldiers', pp. 118-122, two illustrations printed in red and black.
'The Last Hen', pp. 177-181, one illustration printed in green.
Note: the first two stories and illustrations appeared in *The Strand Magazine* in 1916. The third story has been written to make use of one of the illustrations from 'The Rusty Pot and the Wooden Balls' that also appeared in *The Strand Magazine* in 1916.

112. 'Enter Charity' by James Hopper.
Pearson's Magazine, Sep 1918. Vol 46, pp. 150-156.
Two full page and one smaller half-tone illustrations.

113. 'If Our Caricaturists Had Flourished Before!' by Adrian Margaux.
Strand Magazine, Nov 1918. Vol 56, pp. 363-367.
11 illustrations by various artists of which one small line drawing entitled 'The Merry Monarch' is by WHR.

1919

114. **Playbox Annual for 1920**. Amalgamated Press, London, n.d. (1919).
Contains the following stories illustrated by WHR:
'Jack, or the Golden Snuff Box', pp. 53-59, three illustrations printed in black.
'Stupider and Stupider', pp. 118-121, two illustrations in red and black.
Note: These stories and illustrations first appeared in *The Strand Magazine* in 1915.

115. 'The Magic Scooter' by William Caine.
Out and Away Magazine, Jul 1919. Vol 1, pp. 29-36.
Eight small line drawings.

116. 'The Little Folk'.
    The Graphic Christmas Number, 1919. Vol 100, p. 15.
    A full page 'goblin' picture in full colour.

1920

117. **The Cream of Curiosity** by R. L. Hine. G. Routledge & Sons, London, 1920.
    219 × 142 mm. xvi, 416 pp.
    Plum cloth decorated in gilt on front and spine.
    Various illustrations in half-tone printed in sepia on coated paper including two
        full page line drawings by WHR.
    Note: These two illustrations were first published in *The Works of Rabelais* in 1904,
        one appearing on p. 61 of Vol 1 and the other on p. 337 of Vol 1.

118. **Playbox Annual for 1921**. Amalgamated Press, London, n.d. (1920)
    Contains the following stories illustrated by WHR:
    'The Greedy Boy and the Princess', pp. 9-12, two illustrations printed in red and
        black.
    'The Running Broomsticks', pp. 146-149, four illustrations printed in blue.
    Note: The illustrations were first published in *The Strand Magazine*, those to the
        first story having been drawn to illustrate 'The Sea Goblins' (1915) and those
        to the second 'Kill or Cure' (1917). The stories here are new and were written to
        fit the illustrations.

119. **Pelman Pie** edited by Max Pemberton. Hodder & Stoughton for the Pelman
        Institute, London, n.d. (1920).
    278 × 217 mm. 116 pp.
    Pictorial paper wrappers.
    12 coloured plates and numerous line drawings by various artists including a
        'serious' full page coloured lithograph by WHR entitled 'The Mother'.

120. 'Snakes Alive!' by Crosbie Garstin.
    Strand Magazine, Dec 1920. Vol 60, pp. 569-572.
    Two line drawings printed in red and black, one extending across two pages.

121. 'The Old "Visiters"'.
    The Graphic Christmas Number, 1920. Vol 102, p. 9.
    A full page half-tone 'goblin' picture in blue and orange.

1921

122a. **Old Time Stories** told by Master Charles Perrault. Translated from the French by
        A. E. Johnson. Constable & Co. Ltd., London, 1921.
    250 × 182 mm. xii, 200 pp.
    Red cloth blocked in gilt with the design from the pictorial title page on a circular
        white panel on the front and a pictorial design on the spine. Top edge stained
        red.
    Six coloured plates tipped on to beige card mounts, 26 full page and 24 smaller
        line drawings.
  b. Reissued in a binding without the white roundel on the front and with the
        coloured plates on green 'sugar-paper' mounts.

123. **Playbox Annual for 1922**. Amalgamated Press, London, n.d. (1921).
    Contains the following stories with illustrations by WHR:
    'The Three Magicians', pp. 52-55, two illustrations printed in black.
    'The Magic Harp', pp. 145-147, one illustration printed in blue.
    Note: The illustrations first appeared in *The Strand Magazine*. Those to the first
        story illustrated 'The Death of Rancing Roarer' (1914) and that to the second
        illustrated 'One Arabian Night' (1917).

124. 'Treasure Trove' A Poem by W. Gurney Benham.
     Little Folks Magazine, Jul 1921. Vol 94, p. 204.
     One threequarter page line drawing.

125. 'Tight Money' by Stephen Leacock.
     Nash's Pall Mall Magazine, Jul 1921. Vol 67, pp. 377-379.
     Two half-tone illustrations of which one extends across two pages and the other
     is small.

126. 'That Vampire Woman, I Want To Meet Her' by Stephen Leacock.
     Nash's Pall Mall Magazine, Aug 1921. Vol 67, pp. 443-446.
     Three half-tone illustrations of which one extends across two pages, one is half
     page and one is very small.

127. 'The Crime Wave' by Stephen Leacock.
     Nash's Pall Mall Magazine, Sep 1921. Vol 67, pp. 601-603.
     Two half-tone illustrations of which one extends across two pages and the other
     is half page.

128. 'The Moral Wave of the New Year and How to Duck Under It' by Stephen
     Leacock.
     Nash's Pall Mall Magazine, Dec 1921. Vol 68., pp. 230-233.
     Two half-tone illustrations in red and black, one full page and the other extending
     across two pages.

1922

129. **Peter Quip In Search of a Friend** written and illustrated by W. Heath Robinson.
     S. W. Partridge & Co. Ltd., London, n.d. (1922).
     266 × 200 mm. 48 pp.
     Quarter green cloth, red paper covered boards with one of the coloured plates
     reproduced on the front.
     Eight coloured plates, eight half page line drawings, title page vignette and 11
     smaller decorative drawings which are portions of the coloured plates repeated
     in line only.

130. **Ward, Lock Story Books**.
     During 1922 and 1923 the firm of Ward, Lock & Co. published a series of eight
     story books. Each volume was bound in cloth backed pictorial boards and had
     endpapers designed by WHR printed in orange and black showing characters
     from fairy stories on the front endpapers and from nursery rhymes on the back
     endpapers. The titles and publication dates were:
     a. *The "After You" Story Book*. Jun 1922.
     b. *The Fairy Queen Story Book*. Jun 1922.
     c. *The Rainy Day Story Book*. Jun 1922.
     d. *The Sunny Day Story Book*. Jun 1922.
     e. *The Buttercups and Daisies Story Book*. Aug 1922.
     f. *The Summer Days Story Book*. Aug 1922
     g. *The Bedtime Story Book*. Jul 1923.
     h. *The Make-Believe Story Book*. Jul 1923.

131. 'Violent Verse for Patient People, I — Relations'. Anon.
     Royal Magazine, Sep 1922. Vol 48, pp. 412-413.
     Ten small line drawings.

132. 'Violent Verse for Patient People, II — Ladies'. Anon.
     Royal Magazine, Oct 1922. Vol 48, pp. 566-567.
     Ten small line drawings.

133. 'Violent Verse for Patient People, III — Games'. Anon.
     Royal Magazine, Nov 1922. Vol 49, pp. 90-91.

Ten small line drawings.

134. 'The Gold Cup' by W. A. Darlington.
     Pearson's Magazine, Nov 1922. Vol 54, pp. 397-405.
     Four half page line drawings.

1923

135. **Topsy Turvy Tales.** Told by Elsie Smeaton Munro. John Lane The Bodley Head
     Ltd., London, 1923.
     209 × 165 mm. xii, 179 pp.
     Blue cloth decoratively blocked in orange and black.
     Six coloured plates, 16 full page and 20 smaller line drawings.

136. 'The Waits'.
     Holly Leaves, Dec 1923, p. 34.
     A full colour, full page 'goblin' picture.

1924

137. 'The Christmas Robbers'.
     The Graphic Christmas Number, 1924. Vol 110, p. 14.
     A full page, half-tone 'goblin' picture in orange and black.

138. Cover design in full colour and gold: 'Help in the Kitchen'.
     Good Housekeeping, Dec 1924. Vol 6.

1925

139. **Good Housekeeping Cookery Book** by Florence B. Jack.
     Good Housekeeping, London, 1925.
     182 × 124 mm. 254 pp.
     Pale blue cloth titled in navy.
     Full colour dustwrapper design by WHR.
     Note: This design was first used on the cover of *Good Housekeeping Magazine*,
     Dec 1924.

140. 'Old Tales Retold'. A series of six stories by Ben Travers published in *The Passing
     Show* between 3rd Jan and 7th Feb 1925, each with a half page line drawing. The
     titles, dates and page numbers of the individual stories are:
     a. 'Beauty and the Beast'. 3rd Jan, pp. 16-17.
     b. 'Bluebeard'. 10th Jan, pp. 16-17.
     c. 'Aladdin'. 17th Jan, pp. 16-17.
     d. 'Jack and the Beanstalk'. 24th Jan, pp. 20-21.
     e. 'The Babes in the Wood'. 31st Jan, pp. 20-21.
     f. 'Little Red Riding Hood'. 7th Feb, pp. 14-15.

141. 'Misguided Lives'. A series of six stories by Ben Travers published in *The Passing
     Show* between 14th Feb and 21st Mar 1925, each with a three-quarter page
     line drawing. The titles, dates and page numbers of the individual stories are:
     a. 'Antonio'. 14th Feb, pp. 14-15.
     b. 'The Excelsior Tourist'. 21st Feb, pp. 14-15.
     c. 'Hamlet'. 28th Feb, pp. 14-15.
     d. 'Ethelred the Unready'. 7th Mar, pp. 14-15.
     e. 'Leander'. 14th Mar, pp. 14-15.
     f. 'Midas'. 21st Mar, pp. 28-29.

142. 'Spinster's Rest. A Fantasy' by Clemence Dane.
     Nash's Pall Mall Magazine, Sep 1925. Vol 75, pp. 58-59.
     One half-tone illustration filling the upper half of two pages.

143. 'Minding One's Own Business' by Frank Swinnerton.
     Good Housekeeping, Dec 1925. Vol 8, pp. 22-23.

One half-tone illustration in blue and green extending across two pages.

144. 'How I Raised My Own Salary' by Stephen Leacock.
Nash's Pall Mall Magazine, Dec 1925. Vol 76, pp. 10-13.
Ten small half-tone illustrations, five in black and orange and five in blue and orange.
Note: The front cover design for this issue is also by WHR in full colour heightened with gold and shows a jester with two babies.

145. 'The Giant's Shoes' by W. K. Clifford.
Pears Annual, 1925. pp. 32-33.
One full page and two smaller pen and wash drawings in sepia.

146. 'Snowdrop' by Ben Travers.
The Passing Show Christmas Number, 1925. pp. 24-25.
Two half page and one small line drawings.

147. 'The Truth About Grown-Ups — By One Who Knows!'
The Graphic Christmas Number, Nov 1925. Vol 112, p. 14.
A full page half-tone 'goblin' picture in red and black.

148. 'The Fairy's Birthday'.
Holly Leaves, 1925. p. 21.
A full page coloured plate.

1926

149. **Everyland Annual for Boys and Girls. III.** ed. by W. E. Cule. The Carey Press, London, n.d. (1926).
248 × 183 mm. x, 192 pp.
Pictorial red cloth blocked in black and ochre.
Contains the following stories with illustrations by WHR:
a. 'The Camel's Neck', pp. 19-20, one line drawing.
b. 'A Crow is a Crow for Ever', pp. 49-50, one line drawing.
c. 'The Judgement of the Jackal', pp. 83-84, two line drawings and a pictorial initial.
d. 'The Swan and the Crow', pp. 148-150, two line drawings and a pictorial initial.
There is also a small line drawing by WHR on p. 189.
Note: The stories are printed under the collective title 'Fairy Tales of Far Away' by W. H. D. Rouse. They were first published in *The Talking Thrush*, 1899. Two other stories from that book are also reprinted. These two were originally unillustrated and appear here with line drawings by E. Mansell.

150. 'On Giving Way to Things' by Frank Swinnerton.
Nash's Pall Mall Magazine, Mar 1926. Vol 76, pp. 46-47.
Five small half tone illustrations.

151. 'On Thinking Well of Oneself' by Frank Swinnerton.
Good Housekeeping, Apr 1926. Vol 9, pp. 12-13.
Three small half-tone illustrations and a photograph of the author.

152. 'Swank' by Frank Swinnerton.
Good Housekeeping, Nov 1926. Vol 10. pp. 24-25.
One large and three small half-tone illustrations.

153. 'Why Gardeners are Gloomy' by Frank Swinnerton.
Good Housekeeping, Dec 1926. Vol 10, pp. 22-23.
One large drawing extending across two pages and four smaller drawings all in line heightened with green.

154. Cover design in full colour.
Nash's Pall Mall Magazine, Dec 1926. Vol 78.

1927

155. 'What Imagination Will Do — The Noise on the Stair'.
   Pearson's Magazine, Feb 1927. Vol 63, p.165.
   A full page half-tone 'goblin' picture.

156. 'A Sex of Queens' by Clemence Dane.
   Good Housekeeping, Feb 1927. Vol 10, pp.10-11.
   One half-tone illustration filling the upper part of two pages.

157. 'The Duty of Being Agreeable' by Frank Swinnerton.
   Nash's Pall Mall Magazine, Feb 1927. Vol 78, pp.20-21.
   Five small or medium sized half-tone illustrations.

158. 'Tact' by Frank Swinnerton.
   Good Housekeeping, May 1927. Vol 11, pp.16-17.
   Six small half-tone illustrations.

159. 'The Three Bears' by Ben Travers.
   Passing Show Extra Summer Number, 1927. pp.10-11.
   One line drawing extending across two pages.

160. 'Treats' by Frank Swinnerton.
   Good Housekeeping, Aug 1927. Vol 11, pp.12-13.
   Four small or medium sized half-tone illustrations.

161. 'The Advantages of Disaster' by Frank Swinnerton.
   Good Housekeeping, Nov 1927. Vol 12, pp.16-17.
   Six small or medium sized half-tone illustrations.

162. 'Getting Ahead of the Joneses' by R. le Clerc.
   Nash's Pall Mall Magazine, Nov 1927. Vol 80, pp.58-59.
   Four small or medium sized half-tone illustrations.

163. Cover design in full colour — 'Jester Playing Bagpipes'.
   Nash's Pall Mall Magazine, Dec 1927. Vol 80.

164. 'The Fair Day'.
   Holly Leaves, 1927. pp.22-23.
   A double page coloured plate.
   Note: This was first published in *The Studio*, May 1925. (See Appendix C).

1928

165. 'Meals' by Frank Swinnerton.
   Good Housekeeping, Jan 1928. Vol 12, pp.16-17.
   Four small half-tone illustrations.

166. 'Perpetual Romance' by Frank Swinnerton.
   Good Housekeeping, Jul 1928. Vol 13, pp.20-21.
   Five small or medium sized half-tone illustrations.

167. 'Knight Errant of the Post' by Frank Swinnerton.
   Good Housekeeping, Dec 1928. Vol 14, pp.16-17.
   Four line drawings in red and black, of which one extends diagonally across a page
      and the others are small.
   Note: This Christmas issue also has a cover design by WHR in full colour
      heightened with gold, depicting Little Red Riding Hood in the snow carrying
      Christmas fare helped by a number of goblins and a cat.

168. 'Hop-O'-Me-Heart'. A poem by Laurence Housman.
   Nash's Magazine, Dec 1928. Vol 82, pp.40-43.
   Four full page half-tone illustrations with verses inset, two in red and black and
      two in green and black.

169. 'What is the Danger of Christmas?' by A.S. Peake.
     Pall Mall Magazine, Dec 1928. Vol 4 (New series), pp.48-49.
     One half page half-tone illustration in black and white.

170. 'Here We Come Gathering Nuts in May'.
     Holly Leaves, 1928. pp.22-23.
     A double page coloured plate.

1929

171. Cover design in full colour: 'Croquet'.
     Pall Mall Magazine, Jan 1929. Vol 4 (New series).

172. 'Gossip' by Frank Swinnerton.
     Good Housekeeping, Mar 1929. Vol 15, pp.52-53.
     Four small half-tone illustrations.

173. 'The Fun I Get Out of My Garden' by Frank Swinnerton.
     Pall Mall Magazine, Mar 1929. Vol 4 (New series), pp.26-29.
     Three large and three small line drawings.

174. 'The Inconstant Simp' by F.W. Thomas.
     The Passing Show Summer Annual, Jun 1929. pp.12-13.
     One line drawing extending diagonally across one page.

175. 'The Late Queen Anne' by F.W. Thomas.
     The John Bull Summer Annual, Jun 1929. pp.10-11.
     Eight small linked line drawings stretching across the upper parts of two pages.

176. 'Now, If You Take My Advice —' by Helena Normanton.
     Good Housekeeping, Oct 1929. Vol 16, pp.48-49.
     Six small line drawings.

177. 'The Witch Girl' by Phoebe Fenwick Gaye.
     Nash's Pall Mall Magazine, Oct 1929. Vol 84, pp.56-59.
     Two half-tone illustrations, each extending across two pages, one in red and black
       and one in green and black.

178. 'How Novels are Written' by Frank Swinnerton.
     Good Housekeeping, Nov 1929. Vol 16, pp.48-49.
     Six small line drawings.

179. Cover design in full colour and gold — 'The Pedlar'.
     Nash's Pall Mall Magazine, Dec 1929. Vol 84.

180. 'The Enchanter's Daughter' by A.A. Thomson.
     John Bull's Christmas Holiday Annual, Dec 1929. pp.17-18.
     One three-quarter page and one smaller line drawing.

1930

181. 'The Gordian Knot of Domestic Service' by Constance Eaton.
     Good Housekeeping, Feb 1930. Vol 16, pp.48-49.
     Four small or medium sized line drawings.

182. 'Happiness or Freedom' by Clare Sheridan.
     Good Housekeeping, Apr 1930. Vol 17, pp.10-11.
     One half-tone illustration in red and black extending across two pages.

183. '"O". A Scandal of the Court of Queen Elizabeth' by Edward Knoblock.
     Nash's Pall Mall Magazine, Apr 1930. Vol 85, pp.46-49.
     One half-tone illustration in orange and black extending across two pages and one
       in green and black filling two thirds of a page.

184. 'In the Re-Christening of Mary Jane' by Mrs. Aria.
     Good Housekeeping, Jul 1930. Vol 17, pp.56-57.

Two small half-tone and four small line illustrations.

185. 'The Sleeping Beauty' by John Erskine.
     Nash's Pall Mall Magazine, Sep 1930. Vol 85, pp. 16-19.
     One half-tone illustration in blue and black and one in red and black, each
     extending across two pages.

186. 'On Being ·Efficient' by Harold Nicholson.
     Nash's Pall Mall Magazine, Dec 1930. Vol 86, pp. 24-25.
     Six small line drawings.

187. 'The Dragon and the Dowager' by A. A. Thomson.
     John Bull's Christmas Holiday Annual, Nov 1930. pp. 12-13.
     One line drawing extending across two pages and a vignette.

1931

188. **If I Were You** by P. G. Wodehouse. Herbert Jenkins, London, 1931.
     190 × 125 mm. 280 pp.
     Red cloth blocked in black. Full colour pictorial dustwrapper with an illustration
     by WHR.

189. 'Are Authors Human Beings?' by J. B. Priestley.
     Nash's Pall Mall Magazine, Apr 1931. Vol 87, pp. 26-27.
     Six small line drawings.

190. 'The Truth About Ethelred' by A. A. Thomson.
     John Bull's Summer Holiday Annual, 1931. pp. 8-9.
     One line drawing extending across two pages.

191. 'Beds' by Groucho Marx.
     Passing Show Summer Holiday Annual, 1931. pp. 22-23.
     Three medium sized line drawings, of which two have circular frames.

192. 'The Magic Potion' by A. A. Thomson.
     The Passing Show Christmas Number, 1931. pp. 12-13.
     One line drawing extending across two pages.

193. 'The Story of Cocktails' by Anthony Armstrong.
     Strand Magazine, Dec 1931. Vol 82, pp. 621-631.
     Ten half page illustrations, seven circular vignettes and a photograph in orange
     and black half-tone.
     Note: The photograph shows the Knickerbocker bar on the 'Empress of Britain'
     which was decorated with Heath Robinson's paintings of the story of a cocktail.

1932

194a. **Arabian Nights.** The Children's Press, Glasgow, n.d. (1932).
     285 × 210 mm. pp. unnumbered.
     Quarter yellow cloth, pictorial front board and plain grey back board. The spine
     decorated and titled in dark blue.
     Eight coloured plates and numerous line drawings by various artists of which
     two coloured plates, one full page and 24 smaller line drawings are by WHR.
     Note: The two coloured plates by WHR originally appeared as line drawings in
     the 1899 edition, from which all of the line drawings in this book have been
     taken. They have been coloured by another hand.

   b. Reprinted by The Children's Press, n.d., with fewer stories and no coloured
     plates.
     Card wrappers with coloured pictures by Harry Rountree front and back. Line
     drawings by various artists of which two full page and 16 smaller line drawings
     are by WHR. Very poorly printed.

195. 'I'll Tell You Everything'. A nine-part serial by J.B. Priestley and Gerald Bullett. *Nash's Pall Mall Magazine*, Mar-Nov 1932. Vols 88-90.
Mar pp. 6-9, Apr pp. 24-27, May pp. 20-23 and p. 90, Jun pp. 28-31, Jul pp. 26-29 and p. 92, Aug pp. 56-59, Sep pp. 54-57, Oct pp. 42-45, Nov pp. 60-63.
21 half-tone illustrations of which 17 extend across two pages and four are half page. One small decoration in line. Of the large illustrations four are printed in two colours.
Note: The half page illustrations on p. 90 of the May issue and p. 92 of the July issue are parts of larger illustrations that appeared in the March and April issues respectively.

196. 'A Morning Snooze' by W. A. Darlington.
The Passing Show Summer Annual, Jun 1932. pp. 8-10.
One half-tone illustration extending across two pages.

1933

197a. **The Incredible Adventures of Professor Branestawm** by Norman Hunter, John Lane The Bodley Head Ltd., London, 1933.
210×165 mm. xiv, 203 pp. + 4 pp. advertisements.
Orange cloth blocked in blue with the drawing from the half title on the lower front board. Titled in blue on spine and top edge stained blue.
Coloured frontispiece, pictorial title, six full page and 66 smaller line drawings and pictorial endpapers.
Note: Only those drawings with line borders obviously intended to be 'full page' have been counted as such, although a number of other drawings of various sizes have a page to themselves.

b. A new edition published by Penguin Books, Harmondsworth, 1946 in the 'Puffin Story Books' series.
181×111 mm. 208 pp.
Orange and yellow card wrappers with a design incorporating the drawing from the pictorial title page of the first edition. Five full page and 65 smaller line drawings.
Reprinted about twenty times.
The wrapper was changed for later printings.

c. A new edition published by The Bodley Head, London, 1965.
196×135 mm. (viii), 203 pp.
Turquoise blue linson titled in gilt on the spine. Pictorial pink and blue dust-wrapper.
Six full page and 66 smaller line drawings.
Reprinted 1966, 1968, 1971, 1974, 1977, 1979.

198. **The Children's Wonder Book** edited by John R. Crossland and J.M. Parrish. Odham's Press Ltd., London, 1933.
252×175 mm. 768 pp.
Blue pebble grained cloth blocked in blind and titled in gilt, top edge stained blue.
Coloured frontispiece and numerous line drawings of which six are by WHR.
Note: The WHR drawings are to 'Alladin' and 'The Story of the Fisherman' and were first published in the 1899 edition of *The Arabian Nights*.

199. 'What is Happening to Social Standards?' by Rosita Forbes.
Good Housekeeping, Aug 1933. Vol 23, p. 51.
One half page half-tone illustration.

200. 'White Elephants Please' by Christine Jope-Slade.
Pearson's Magazine, Sep 1933. Vol 76, pp. 248-254.

Three half-tone illustrations of which two extend across two pages and the third is smaller.

201. 'Miss Francis Goes to Stay With Friends' by Richmal Crompton.
Good Housekeeping, Nov 1933. Vol 24, pp. 6-9.
Two half-tone illustrations each extending across two pages, one in red and black.

202. 'Night Fears'. A poem by Laurence Housman.
Nash's Pall Mall Magazine, Nov 1933. Vol 92, pp. 22-23.
One pen and wash illustration in blue and black extending across two pages.

203. 'The Wedding Feast'.
Holly Leaves, Nov 1933. pp. 22-23.
A double page full colour picture.

204. 'Sir Borloys and the Dark Knight' by Anthony Armstrong.
Strand Magazine, Dec 1933. Vol 86, pp. 634-643.
Four half-tone illustrations in orange and black, of which three extend across two pages and one diagonally across one page, and a pictorial initial.

205. 'Whittington's Cat'. A story by Lady Eleanor Smith.
Radio Times, 22nd Dec 1933. Vol 41, pp. 864-867, 880.
Headpiece and two quarter page illustrations in line.

1934

206. **Balbus. A Latin reading book for junior forms** by George Maxwell Lyne. E. Arnold & Co., London, 1934.
174 × 112 mm. 128 pp.
Blue cloth with a pictorial design blocked in gilt on the front and titled in gilt on the front and spine.
Four full page and four smaller line drawings and two vignettes. One of the smaller line drawings is repeated on the title page and on the front cover.

207. **Heath Robinson's Book of Goblins**. Stories from Vernaleken's *In the Land of Marvels*. Hutchinson & Co. (Publishers) Ltd., London, n.d. (1934).
244 × 184 mm. 239 pp.
Dark blue morocco grained cloth blocked in blind with a pictorial design on the front and spine. Titled in gilt on front and spine.
Seven coloured plates, eight full page and 45 smaller line drawings and 93 vignettes of goblins.
Also issued in a 'de Luxe' binding of simulated green leather with gilt edges.

208. 'Seaman's Prayer'. A poem by John Masefield.
Nash's Pall Mall Magazine, Jul 1934. Vol 93, pp. 22-23.
One double page half-tone illustration in orange and black with the verse inset.

209. 'Wisdom and Wedding Presents' by Quentin Robinson.
Pearson's Magazine, Jul 1934. Vol 78, pp. 40-44.
Headpiece extending across two pages and twelve small drawings in half-tone.

210. 'Dickens is not Dead' by John Van Druten.
Nash's Pall Mall Magazine, Sep 1934. Vol 93, pp. 22-25.
Two half-tone illustrations each extending across two pages, one in red and black and the other in blue and black.

211. 'Village Revels'.
Holly Leaves, Nov 1934. pp. 20-21.
A double page full colour picture.

212. 'Christmas and the Gardener' by Beverley Nichols.
Good Housekeeping, Dec 1934. Vol 26, pp. 22-23.

Four small line drawings in red and black.

213. 'Worlds Without End' by Dr. H. Spencer Jones.
Nash's Pall Mall Magazine, Dec 1934. Vol 94, pp. 20-21.
One half-tone illustration in green and black extending across two pages.

1935

214. 'Science Sets the Pace' by Gerald Heard.
Nash's Pall Mall Magazine, Jan 1935. Vol 94, pp. 6-7.
Double page design incorporating a large headpiece flanked by eight small pictures, all in half-tone, in red and black.

215. 'The Lamp of God' by Ellery Queen.
Nash's Pall Mall Magazine, Jun 1935. Vol 95, pp. 6-11.
One half-tone illustration in orange and black extending across two pages by WHR. Other illustrations by M. Mackinlay.

216. 'Food For Thought — A Brief Survey of the Autumn Talks'. Anon.
Radio Times, 27th Sep 1935. Vol 48, pp. 6-7.
Four small line drawings.

217. 'The Valiant Little Tailor' by Clemence Dane.
Nash's Pall Mall Magazine, Oct 1935. Vol 96., pp. 30-36.
Four half-tone illustrations of which three extend across two pages and the other is a vignette. Two of the larger drawings in red and black, the others in black and white.

218. 'Methods of Approach' by Michael Harrison.
Good Housekeeping, Nov 1935. Vol 28, pp. 12-15.
Three half-tone illustrations of which two extend across two pages and the other is small. One of the large illustrations is in black and white, the other two are in blue and black.

219. 'At Home With Heath Robinson' by K. R. G. Browne.
Strand Magazine, Nov 1935. Vol 90, pp. 66-72.
Ten half-tone illustrations of various sizes.

220. 'Queen of the South' by Clemence Dane.
Nash's Pall Mall Magazine, Dec 1935. Vol 96, pp. 64-73.
One full page and one vignette half-tone illustrations in orange and black.

221. Design for contents page.
Radio Times Christmas Number, 1935. p. 1.
A border of small linked line drawings.

222. 'The Toast'.
Holly Leaves, Nov 1935. pp. 24-25.
A double page full colour picture.

1936

223a. **How To Live In a Flat** by Heath Robinson and K. R. G. Browne. Hutchinson & Co. (Publishers), Ltd., London, n.d. (1936).
185 × 120 mm. viii, 128 pp.
Orange pictorial cloth blocked in black. Top edge stained orange. Pictorial dust-wrapper in blue and black.
40 full page and 79 smaller line drawings. Pictorial endpapers printed in black on grey paper.

  b. Reissued in blue cloth printed in black, n.d.

  c. A facsimile reprint from Duckworth, 1976.

216 × 131 mm. vi, 128 pp.
Black linson titled in gilt on the spine, pictorial dustwrapper.
Illustrated as the first edition, slightly enlarged.

224. 'The Man Who Could Work Miracles' by H. G. Wells.
Nash's Pall Mall Magazine, Jan 1936. Vol 96, pp. 107-128.
Six half-tone illustrations including one full page in blue and black, two double page in red and black and three smaller.

225. 'The Truth About Mrs. Brown' by V. S. Pritchett.
Nash's Pall Mall Magazine, Mar 1936. Vol 96, pp. 111-127.
Five half-tone illustrations of which one is full page, three extend across two pages and one is a small circular vignette. Of the larger drawings two are in orange and black and two are in green and black.

226. 'Down With the Fussers' by Warwick Deeping.
Good Housekeeping, Apr 1936. Vol 29, pp. 10-11.
Three half-tone illustrations of which one extends across two pages and two are smaller.

227. 'The Face of Wax' by Edith Pargeter.
Good Housekeeping, Dec 1936. Vol 30, pp. 14-17.
Two half-tone illustrations extending across two pages, one in green and black and one in red and black, and a vignette in red and black.

228. 'Mascot for Uncle' by A. J. Cronin.
Nash's Pall Mall Magazine, Dec 1936. Vol 98, pp. 18-25.
Six illustrations in half-tone including a one-and-a-half page drawing in red and black, one across two pages in green and black, one half page drawing, and three smaller drawings.

1937

229a. **How to Be a Perfect Husband** by W. Heath Robinson and K. R. G. Browne. Hutchinson & Co. (Publishers), Ltd., London, n.d. (1937).
184 × 119 mm. (vi), 130 pp.
Turquoise pictorial cloth printed in black. Pictorial dustwrapper in yellow and black. Top edge stained turquoise.
31 full page and 86 smaller line drawings. Pictorial endpapers in turquoise on white.

   b. Reissued in blue cloth printed in black, n.d.

   c. A facsimile reprint from Duckworth, 1976.
216 × 131 mm. vi, 130pp.
Black linson titled in gilt on the spine, pictorial dustwrapper.
Illustrated as the first edition, slightly enlarged.

230. 'Circus' cover design.
Radio Times, 31st Dec 1937.
Full page line drawing.

1938

231a. **How to Make a Garden Grow** by Heath Robinson and K. R. G. Browne. Hutchinson & Co. (Publishers), Ltd., London, n.d. (1938).
187 × 118 mm. viii, 104 pp.
Green pictorial cloth printed in black. Pictorial dustwrapper in green and black. Top edge stained green.
15 full page and 100 smaller line drawings. Pictorial endpapers in brown on cream.

   b. Reissued in dull blue cloth, n.d. (ca. 1946).

    c. Facsimile reprint by Duckworth, 1980.
       216 × 131 mm. vi, 104 pp.
       Black linson titled in gilt on the spine, pictorial dustwrapper.
       Illustrations as first edition, slightly enlarged.

232a. **My Line of Life** by W. Heath Robinson. Blackie & Son Ltd., London, 1938.
      246 × 184 mm. (xii), 198 pp.
      Ochre cloth blocked in brown with a pictorial design, and titled in brown on the front and spine. Pictorial dustwrapper.
      Three full page photographs, one half-tone plate and 78 smaller line drawings first published in this book, together with 12 full page half-tone plates, 11 full page and 23 smaller line drawings previously published elsewhere.

    b. A facsimile reprint by E. P. Publishing, Wakefield, 1974. Bound in red simulated leather titled in gilt on the spine. Pictorial dustwrapper printed in black, silver and green.

233. **Success With Stocks and Shares** by John B. Gledhill and Frank Preston. Sir Isaac Pitman and Sons Ltd., London, 1938.
     211 × 137 mm. xi, 138 pp. + 32 pp. advertisements.
     Stone coloured cloth blocked in black with a small pictorial design on the front.
     Four full page line drawings.

234. 'Women are Motherly' by Sir Hugh Walpole.
     Good Housekeeping, May 1938. Vol 33, pp. 6-9.
     Two illustrations extending across two pages of which one is in red and black, and a vignette, all in half-tone.

235. 'A Highly Complicated Science' by K. R. G. Browne.
     Strand Magazine, Aug 1938. Vol 95, pp. 395-399.
     Nine line drawings.
     Note: These drawings were subsequently used in *How to Make a Garden Grow* with different captions, generally shorter.

236. 'Halcyon Ghosts'. A Christmas fancy by S. P. B. Mais.
     Radio Times, 23rd Dec 1938. pp. 26-27.
     Six small line drawings.

1939

237a. **How To Be a Motorist** by Heath Robinson and K. R. G. Browne. Hutchinson & Co. (Publishers), Ltd., London, n.d. (1939).
      185 × 118 mm. x, 116 pp.
      Red pictorial cloth blocked in black. Pictorial dustwrapper in red and black. Top edge stained red.
      Five full page and 104 smaller line drawings. Pictorial endpapers printed in black on cream.

    b. Reissued in dull blue cloth, n.d.

    c. Facsimile reprint by Duckworth, 1977.
      216 × 131 mm. vi, 116 pp.
      Black linson titled in gilt on the spine, pictorial dustwrapper. Illustrations as first edition, slightly enlarged.

238. **Professor Branestawm Stories** by Norman Hunter. E. J. Arnold and Son Ltd., Leeds, Glasgow & Belfast, n.d. (1939).
     No. 27 in the 'Broadcast Echoes' Series.
     180 × 128 mm. 96 pp.
     Cream card wrappers decorated in red and blue.
     11 line drawings of which two full page and four smaller ones are by WHR.

Note: Five of the eight stories in the book are from *The Incredible Adventures of Professor Branestawm* (1933) where the Heath Robinson illustrations first appeared. The other three stories are illustrated by another artist.

239. 'Motoring Hints'. A series of six articles by K. R. G. Browne and W. Heath Robinson published in *Illustrated Magazine* from 8th April to 13th May 1939. The individual articles were:
a. 'How a Car Works', 8th Apr, pp. 45-46, six small line drawings.
b. 'How to Chose a Car', 15th Apr, pp. 34-35, eight small line drawings.
c. 'How to Drive a Car', 22nd Apr, p. 30, three small line drawings.
d. 'Maintenance and Simple Repairs', 29th Apr, p. 40, four small line drawings.
e. 'Road Sense and Etiquette', 6th May, p. 40, two small line drawings and five vignettes of road signs.
f. 'Special Bodies', 13 May, p. 40, six small line drawings.
Note: The six articles became the first six chapters of *How to Be a Motorist*. All of the illustrations were used in that book.

1940

240. **Mein Rant** by R. F. Patterson. Blackie & Son Ltd., London, 1940.
195 × 131 mm. x, 70 pp.
Light brown cloth titled in dark brown.
Six full page and six half page line drawings.

241a. **How To Make the Best of Things** by W. Heath Robinson and Cecil Hunt. Hutchinson & Co. (Publishers), Ltd., London, n.d. (1940).
185 × 119 mm. viii, 120 pp.
Blue pictorial cloth blocked in black. Pictorial dustwrapper in mauve and black.
Ten full page and 114 smaller line drawings. Pictorial endpapers in black on mauve.

b. Facsimile reprint by Duckworth, 1981.
216 × 131 mm. vi, 120 pp.
Black linson titled in gilt on the spine, pictorial dustwrapper.
Illustrations as for the first edition, slightly enlarged.

242. 'Mediterranean Blitzkrieg?' by George Slocombe.
Illustrated Magazine, 13th Jul 1940. pp. 19-22.
One pen and wash drawing extending across two pages.

1941

243a. **How to Build a New World** by W. Heath Robinson and Cecil Hunt. Hutchinson & Co. (Publishers), Ltd., London, n.d. (1941).
185 × 118 mm. viii, 136 pp.
Orange pictorial cloth printed in black. Pictorial dustwrapper in yellow and black.
Two double page, 16 full page and 117 smaller line drawings.
Pictorial endpapers printed in brown.

b. Reissued in blue cloth, n.d.

c. Facsimile reprint by Duckworth, 1981.
216 × 131 mm. vi, 136 pp.
Black linson titled in gilt on the spine. Pictorial dustwrapper.
Illustrations as first edition, slightly enlarged.

244. 'I Saw Yesterday' by Irene Veal.
Radio Times, 19th Sep 1941. Vol 72, p. 4.
One small line drawing.

1942

245a. 'Cranford Ladies'. A radio play adapted by Jane Stratton from Mrs. Gaskell, details of the broadcast of which are given in
Radio Times, 13th Feb 1942. Vol 74, p. 6 accompanied by
One small line drawing entitled 'Miss Matty'.

 b. The illustration was reprinted in Radio Times, 20th Jun 1952. Vol 115, p. 8 when the play was repeated.

246. 'The Vicar's Temptation'.
Holly Leaves, Nov 1942. p. 6.
A full page coloured plate.

1943

247a. **How To Run a Communal Home** by W. Heath Robinson and Cecil Hunt. Hutchinson & Co. (Publishers), Ltd., London, n.d. (1943).
182 × 120 mm. viii, 116 pp.
Red pictorial cloth printed in black. Pictorial dustwrapper in dull yellow and black.
Six double page, 13 full page and 107 smaller line drawings.
Pictorial endpapers in black and white.

 b. Facsimile reprint by Duckworth, 1980.
216 × 131 mm. vi, 116 pp.
Black linson titled in gilt on the spine. Pictorial dustwrapper.
Illustrations as first edition, slightly enlarged.

248. 'Christmas Scandal'.
Holly Leaves, Nov 1943. p. 10.
A full page coloured plate.

1944

249. **Once Upon a Time** by Liliane M. C. Clopet. Frederick Muller Ltd., London, 1944.
187 × 121 mm. 108 pp.
Green cloth titled in black on the spine. Pictorial dustwrapper in green, orange and black.
12 full page and 31 smaller line illustrations.

250. 'Every Elf and Fairy Sprite...'
Holly Leaves, Nov 1944. p. 10.
A full page coloured plate illustrating four lines of verse from 'A Midsummer Night's Dream'.

1946

251. **The Enchanted Isle**. Music for violin and piano composed by Walter Carroll. Forsyth Brothers Ltd., London, n.d. (1946).
310 × 242 mm. 16 pp. + 4 pp. violin parts loosely inserted.
Front cover and title drawings in line.

1953

252. **The Adventures of Don Quixote de la Mancha** by Miguel de Cervantes. J. M. Dent & Sons Ltd., London, 1953 in the 'Children's Illustrated Classics' series.
210 × 134 mm. x, 371 pp.
Beige cloth printed with a repeating design in green, matching endpapers. Titled in black on the front and spine, top edge stained dark grey. Pictorial dustwrapper.

Eight coloured plates and 26 full page line drawings.

Reprinted 1956.

Note: The coloured plates and ten of the line drawings are first published in this edition. The remaining 16 line drawings are taken from the 1902 edition published by Dent.

1962

253. **Perrault's Complete Fairy Tales**. Translated from the French by A. E. Johnson and Others. Constable, London, 1962.

232 × 154 mm. viii, 184 pp.

Blue linson blocked in gilt with a design of a coach and horses on the front and titled in gilt on the spine. Pale blue dustwrapper with a coloured illustration on the front.

26 full page and 17 smaller line drawings and five vignettes.

Reprinted four times by Penguin Books under the Kestrel imprint.

Note: All of the illustrations are taken from *Old Time Stories* (1921), the frontispiece from that book being reproduced on the dustwrapper. This book however contains three additional stories, which are not illustrated, and also has morals added to all of the stories.

1978

254a. **Goblins**. Verses by Spike Milligan. Illustrations by W. Heath Robinson. Hutchinson of London, 1978.

153 × 116 mm. pp. unnumbered (60 pp.).

Brown linson blocked with a pictorial design in gilt on the front. Full colour pictorial dustwrapper.

39 illustrations printed in black and two colours.

Note: All of the illustrations are taken from the vignettes in *Heath Robinson's Book of Goblins*.

b. Reprinted 1980 and issued in pictorial wrappers by Arrow Books.

1979

255. **The Heath Robinson Illustrated Story Book**. The Hamlyn Publishing Group Ltd., 1979 under the Beaver Books imprint.

241 × 183 mm. 96 pp.

Pale blue pictorial card wrappers.

33 line drawings of which 18 extend across two pages.

Note: The stories and illustrations have all been taken from the *Playbox Annuals* for the years 1917 to 1922. All of the illustrations were first published in *The Strand Magazine* between 1914 and 1917, some of them illustrating different stories from the ones reprinted in this book.

Appendix A

Books of Humorous Drawings Published During Heath Robinson's Lifetime.

1. *Some 'Frightful' War Pictures*. Duckworth, 1915.
2. *Hunlikely!* Duckworth, 1916.
3. *The Saintly Hun*. Duckworth, n.d. (1917).
4. *Flypapers*. Duckworth, 1919.
5. *Get On With It*. G. Heath Robinson & J. Birch, n.d. (1920).
6. *A Jamboree of Laughter from a Boy Scout's Diary*. A.V.N. Jones, n.d. (1920).
7. *The Home Made Car*. Duckworth, n.d. (1921).
8. *Motor Mania*. 'The Motor Owner', n.d. (1921).
9. *Quaint and Selected Pictures*. G. Heath Robinson & J. Birch, n.d. (1922).
10. *Humours of Golf*. Methuen, 1923.
11. *Absurdities*. Hutchinson, n.d. (1934).
12. *Railway Ribaldry*. Great Western Railway, 1935.
13. *Let's Laugh*. Hutchinson, n.d. (1939).
14. *Heath Robinson at War*. Methuen, 1942.

Appendix B

Summary Table of Illustrations and Cartoons in Magazines

● Illustrations   O Cartoons   ◐ Illustrations and Cartoons

Name of Magazine
The Aeroplane
The Bystander
Flying
Good Housekeeping
Grand
The Graphic
Holly Leaves
The Humorist
Hutchinson's Magazine
Illustrated
The Illustrated Sporting & Dramatic News
John Bull
Lady's Realm
Little Folks
London Magazine
London Opinion
The Magpie
Nash's Magazine*
Out and Away
Pall Mall Magazine
Passing Show
Pearson's Magazine
Piccadilly
Punch
The Quiver
The Radio Times
The Royal Magazine
The Sketch
The Strand Magazine
Sunday Reading for the Young
The Sunday Graphic
The Sunday Magazine
The Tatler
Television Magazine
Tit-Bits
The Windsor Magazine
The Wireless Magazine

* Including Nash's Pall Mall Magazine.

Appendix C

A Select Bibliography of Articles and Books about W. Heath Robinson

1. 'Mr. W. Heath Robinson and His Work'. Anon.
   Strand Magazine, Jul 1908. Vol 36, 41-49.
   Photograph and 14 illustrations, most of which were not published elsewhere.
2. 'Photographic Interviews No. V — A Famous "Sketch" Artist: Mr. W. Heath
   Robinson'.
   The Sketch, 4th Jan 1911. Vol 72, 399-400.
   Seven photographs.
3. **W. Heath Robinson** by A. E. Johnson. Adam and Charles Black, London, 1913 in
   the 'Brush, Pen and Pencil' series.
   216 × 150 mm. viii, 52 pp.
   Beige cloth blocked in black with a pictorial design.
   Seven coloured plates, eight half-tone plates, 16 full page and 31 smaller line
   drawings. A number of these drawings are not published elsewhere.
   Reprinted in 1930.
4. 'The Line Drawings of W. Heath Robinson' by A. E. Johnson.
   The Studio, May 1916. Vol 67, pp. 223-238.
   One double page, six full page and 13 smaller line drawings.
5. **The Art of the Illustrator: W. Heath Robinson and His Work** by Percy V. Bradshaw.
   The Press Art School, London, n.d. (1916).
   340 × 218 mm. 16 pp. text.
   Contained in grey card folder.
   Sepia photograph with humorous line border and six plates tipped on to loose grey
   card mounts showing different stages of the same coloured illustration.
6. 'In the Days of My Youth' by W. Heath Robinson.
   T. P.'s and Cassell's Weekly, 18th Apr 1925. Vol 3, pp. 956, 964 and 966.
   One small line drawing.
7. 'The Art of Mr. Heath Robinson' by A. L. Baldry.
   The Studio, May 1925. Vol 89, pp. 242-249.
   Two full page coloured plates, two full page and one half page half-tone illus-
   trations and one full page and two small drawings in line.
8. 'Joking Apart' by Fenn Sherie.
   Pearson's Magazine, Dec 1930. Vol 70, pp. 579-585.
   Includes one half page half-tone illustration and one small drawing in line and tone
   by WHR, both printed in red and blue.
   The article shows the serious side of six humorous artists.
9. **My Line of Life** by W. Heath Robinson. Blackie & Son Ltd., London, 1938.
   Facsimile Reprint by E. P. Publishing, Wakefield, 1974.
   For details see main Bibliography.

10. 'The Gadget King' by G. W. Langston Day.
    Everybody's Weekly, 31st Mar 1945, pp. 8-9.
    Six half-tone illustrations in red and black, all from the Memorial Exhibition at the Fine Art Society.

11. **The Life and Art of W. Heath Robinson** by G. Langston Day. Herbert Joseph Limited, London, 1947.
    217 × 136 mm. 270 pp.
    Red cloth titled in gilt. Pictorial dustwrapper.
    One double page and six full page coloured plates, three photographs, eight half-tone plates, eight full page and 17 smaller line drawings.
    Reprinted by E. P. Publishing, Wakefield, 1976.

12. **The Penguin W. Heath Robinson**. Introduced by R. Jordan. Penguin Books Ltd., Middlesex, 1966.
    198 × 130mm. pages unnumbered (96pp).
    Pictorial card covers.
    80 full page and five smaller illustrations.

13. 'Magic in His Madness' by Leslie Garner.
    The Sunday Times Magazine, 4th Jun 1972. front cover and pp. 14-22.
    Composite cover design and nine illustrations including a fine example of one of WHR's serious watercolours reproduced in colour.

14. **Heath Robinson, Artist and Comic Genius** by John Lewis, with an introduction by Nicolas Bentley. Constable, London, 1973.
    254 × 180mm. 224pp.
    Green cloth blocked in gilt on the front and spine. Pictorial dustwrapper.
    Four coloured plates, 33 half tone illustrations and 119 drawings in line.

Index

Note: Entries appearing in the Bibliography are indexed by their serial numbers and are in bold type. Similarly, entries appearing in the Appendices are also in bold type, with the appropriate Appendix letter added. Pages containing illustrations are in italics.